Survive the Modern World

How to
THINK
like an
ACTIVIST

Wendy Syfret

Hardie Grant

BOOKS

Introduction

First of all, thank you for picking up *How to Think Like an Activist* and congratulations on starting your activist journey. As you'll soon discover, becoming involved in this kind of work can be hugely rewarding. Behind all the issues and actions are a history and community that are both rich and complex. No book could speak to every part of activist culture, so view this one as the first step.

Across these pages we'll explore the various parts of activism, how different approaches can deliver different results and what activism means to us as individuals. We'll also look at how we can build healthy attitudes, practices and values that will allow us to sustain this work over a lifetime.

While much of the advice in this book is about getting started, our eyes will always be on the future to build activist careers that are long, happy, rewarding and maybe even world-changing.

Chapter One

THE *Unbroken* Line of ACTIVISM

How activism made the modern world

You don't need to look far back into history to see how activism created the world we live in today. Every right, liberty and security we have exists because someone stood up and fought for it. But yesterday's actions didn't only secure the freedoms we currently hold, they also influenced and inspired protest movements that are still raging today. Past activists pioneered new ways of thinking about society, each other and ourselves, as well as creating the resistance strategies we will discuss in this book. We can pay our respects to those brave individuals by studying their achievements, learning from them, and carrying on their world-changing work now and into the future.

The French Revolution

It has been over 200 years since Parisian craftsmen and store owners stormed the Bastille (the fortress being used as a state prison by King Louis XVI) on 14 July 1789. That act of defiance against the monarchy's brutal authoritarian rule set in motion the events that we now know as the French Revolution. At the time, the rebels couldn't have foreseen how their fight to allow French citizens more agency in governmental decisions would change the way people around the world defined and valued equality for centuries to come.

But such far-reaching cultural, political and intellectual change doesn't come easy. The resulting revolution was bloody, leading to a decade of violent turmoil and the execution of thousands of people – including King Louis and Queen Marie Antoinette.

By the close of the 18th century the revolution and stand against nobility resulted in the establishment of a French republic and the end of the monarchy. The revolutionaries' demands for liberty, equality and fraternity rang out beyond their borders and drove ordinary citizens across Europe to begin to challenge their own monarchs. Today the French Revolution is widely seen as a major catalyst in the rise of democracy across the European continent and the beginning of the Age of Revolution. This period of history saw uprisings in Ireland, Haiti and Italy, and across Spanish and Portuguese colonies in Latin America.

The Salt March

Over a century later, Mahatma Gandhi led another stand against oppressive rule. This time the people of India were rebelling against British colonialism. Gandhi's methods were considerably less violent than those used in France, but just as the French revolutionaries inspired a wave of change, he also popularised a new form of peaceful protests.

In March 1930 the lawyer, politician, social activist and writer led thousands of Indians on a 387-kilometre walk from his religious retreat near Ahmedabad to the Arabian Sea coast. The marchers were specifically protesting the British Salt Act of 1882, which banned Indians from collecting and selling salt. When Gandhi eventually reached the sea, he leant down and picked up a small lump of natural salt, breaking the law but not committing any act of violence.

Still, that simple gesture stood as a sign of resistance, inspired millions of people across India and led to a wave of civil disobedience. During this period Gandhi was arrested – along with nearly 60,000 people.

When he was released from prison, Gandhi negotiated with the British to end the ongoing civil unrest in exchange for a role in negotiating India's future at an upcoming conference in London. Those negotiations eventually led to India being granted independence from Britain in 1947. It was not only a win for Indians, and a blow to English colonial rule, but it also demonstrated that nonviolent action could create real change.

Many other world-altering movements can be traced back to the peaceful Salt March. Between 1987 and 1991 Baltic people across Estonia, Latvia and Lithuania called for independence from Soviet domination. Being committed to nonviolence, citizens chose to sing patriotic hymns as a form of protest – resulting in the title the Singing Revolution. During the same period, the 1989 Monday Demonstrations saw a series of peaceful protests held across East Germany. Participants standing against the communist regime gathered under the slogans 'Keine Gewalt' (No violence) and 'Wir sind das Volk' (We are the people). The inclusive and peaceful nature of these gatherings allowed for the movement to balloon in size over several weeks, eventually ending with the fall of the Berlin Wall on 9 November 1989, symbolising for many the end of communism in Eastern Europe and of the Cold War.

 **ACTION**

Create a watch list

There is a lot to be learned from past movements and individuals.
Set yourself a challenge of becoming better acquainted with the
leaders who went before you by committing to watching one
documentary a week on the history of your cause.

Present your case to one person

One of the most effective ways to engage another person in a cause
is to reach out and explain to them what this issue means to you. Look
around – is there anyone in your life who you would like to share your
activism journey with? Maybe it's a partner who you want to invite
into a new part of your life. Or a parent who doesn't quite seem to be
on the same page when thinking of the future.

Make an effort to reach out to them, grab a coffee or go for a walk,
and explain why you're inspired to take a stand on this issue. While it
pays to explain the larger context, be sure to also outline how you are
personally impacted. Often these individual perspectives can make
huge issues feel more accessible.

History alive today

Many of today's most well-known movements can be seen as descendants of previous actions, demonstrating how social and political missions can change and evolve over generations. One of the clearest examples of this is how the history of feminism is often described in waves.

First-wave feminism refers to the suffragette movement of the late 19th and early 20th centuries, which demanded women be awarded the right to vote. In a move that echoes the 2017 Women's March, US suffragettes organised one of their most famous parades in Washington DC on 3 March 1913 – the day before the inauguration of President Woodrow Wilson. Seven years later, the work of those protesters (and thousands of others across the country) led to the ratification of the 19th amendment, awarding women the right to vote.

While the vote was secured, the reality was it wasn't always guaranteed, especially for women of colour. It also didn't represent a total revolution for the rights of women. In the century since, women have continued to follow (sometimes literally) in the footsteps of the suffragettes.

The term second-wave feminism came from a 1968 *New York Times* article, 'The Second Feminist Wave' by Martha Weinman Lear. She wrote: 'Proponents call it the Second Feminist Wave, the first having ebbed after the glorious victory of suffrage and disappeared, finally, into the great sandbar of Togetherness'. While Lear named it, the second wave is often dated from the publication of Betty Friedan's book *The Feminine Mystique* in 1963.

Second-wave feminism has become known for a focus on systemic sexism, gender pay inequality, reproductive freedom and access to education. Here, again, protests and marches were a huge part of the culture. The Take Back the Night events and marches that were held across the 1970s to draw attention to violence against women were particularly influential.

Third-wave feminism is less defined, but refers to the feminist movement of the early 1990s. During this time music played a huge part in activism with the rise of riot grrl groups such as Bikini Kill, Sleater-Kinney, Bratmobile and Heavens to Betsy (among many, many more), who expressed their frustration with sexism through their art. It also saw a greater focus on intersectionality, and a growing acknowledgment that mainstream feminism had historically been overwhelmingly white, cisgender and middle class.

The current fourth wave sees women fighting for many of the same issues. But as the Me Too movement shows, much of the organising and activism has now moved online. The influence of the original feminist activists is still visible, however. Just as the suffragettes marched on Washington DC, several generations later women once again descended on the US capital for the first Women's March in 2017.

Right here, right now

Clearly, activism has always relied on the voices, vision and energy of individuals to inspire and drive social change. We have seen that many of the movements that shaped the world we live in today were begun by people acting alone. Often hardly old enough to vote, they were prepared to take a stand for what they believed in. Now, barely two decades into the 21st century, it's clear that the new millennium will also be shaped by single, disrupting voices ready to prove that no system or establishment is untouchable.

Right now we're living through one of the most complex and volatile periods in recent memory. People from all over the world are confronting issues such as climate change, racial injustice, xenophobia, and violence against women, people of colour and non-binary individuals. All of these causes have been impacted by the social and financial fallout of COVID-19 and the resulting shutdowns. As we emerge from this world-changing event, it's time to come together to confront the reality that the ways we have been living are not sustainable, and the solutions that have been offered don't go far enough. This is a fresh start and it's up to us all to ask: how can we fight to ensure that our deeply altered society will be safer, kinder, stronger and more committed to positive change?

As groups like Black Lives Matter, March for Our Lives and Fridays for Future have shown, you don't need to be a power holder or career activist to change the way we view the world. A fresh generation of activists are transforming the way we fight for what's right. Powered by the internet, nurtured by a vital network of mentors, and increasingly committed to diversity and intersectionality, they're succeeding in capturing public attention, and changing minds and attitudes at a scale never witnessed before.

Yes, the news can be intimidating and the weight of the world overwhelming. It's human to look over all the issues and causes that require attention and feel that one person could never make a difference. But by making the first commitment to ourselves, that we're going to get involved, and working within our own communities, we are able to inspire and support others and create real change. No one person can save the world. But every one of us can shape it.

 **EXPLAINER**

March for Our Lives and the power of teens

March for Our Lives was founded by the survivors of the 2018 school shooting at Marjory Stoneman Douglas High School in Parkland, Florida. In the aftermath of the tragic event, students gathered together and vowed: 'We cannot allow one more person to be killed by senseless gun violence. We cannot allow one more person to experience the pain of losing a loved one. We cannot allow one more family to wait for a call or a text that never comes. We cannot allow the normalization of gun violence to continue'.

This call to action began with a handful of founding members, but immediately resonated with millions of young people around the country who have grown up during a time of escalating school shootings. March for Our Lives is committed to effecting large-scale change within the United States' gun culture by actioning a six-part set of demands:

* Change the standards of gun ownership.
* Halve the rate of gun deaths in 10 years.
* Create accountability for the gun lobby and industry.
* Name a director of gun violence prevention.
* Generate community-based solutions.
* Empower the next generation.

ADULTS LIKE US when we have strong test scores, but they hate us when we have STRONG OPINIONS *

Emma González

The power of youth

Right now, about 41 per cent of the world's population is 24 year old or younger. A staggering 26 per cent are under 15. In Africa, that figure jumps to over 40 per cent. Each month in India, one million people turn 18 and reach voting age. Viewed like that, it's impossible to ignore the collective and growing presence of young people. No matter what happens in the future, there's no denying that we're on the precipice of a huge power shift. You only need to look at the news to witness the world already being remade within this new vision. Individuals from Hong Kong to Chile have begun pressing back on the social structures created by and for their parents and grandparents.

As young activists come of age, they're bringing the issues that matter most to them to a global stage. Major dialogues around topics like authoritarianism, climate justice, gun control and transgender rights are beginning in classrooms, not boardrooms.

In her paper 'The Broader Importance of #FridaysForFuture', which examines the ongoing impact of the global school strike for climate movement, American sociologist Dr Dana R. Fisher reflects: 'This growing movement is important beyond its potential impact on climate policy because it is creating a cohort of citizens who will be active participants in democracy'. As the kids and teens holding placards in the streets move to holding ballots in voting booths, their values are going to transform the countries they live in.

# EXPLAINER

The lasting impact of the March on Washington

On 28 August 1963, more than 200,000 protesters took part in the March on Washington. The event was a collective effort organised by a number of major civil rights organisations, including the Negro American Labor Council, the Southern Christian Leadership Conference, the Congress of Racial Equality and the Student Nonviolent Coordinating Committee. While each group had their own key focus, they joined together to fight for the rights of all African Americans. Collectively they called for the creation of a 'comprehensive civil rights bill' that would address employment, voting rights, access to housing, segregation, systematic disenfranchisement, and discrimination.

Reverend Martin Luther King Jr was invited to speak at the march, and during the event he delivered his iconic 'I Have a Dream' speech. While the protest was focused on the lives of African Americans, marchers included people from all across American society: students, religious leaders, non-unionised domestic workers, Indigenous activists and celebrities. The march coincided with the rise of TV ownership, meaning thousands of people also witnessed it from home.

Prior to the march, President John F. Kennedy met with civil rights leaders to suggest it was ill-timed and to express his concern that it could turn violent. In response Reverend King said, 'Frankly, I have never engaged in any direct-action movement which did not seem ill-timed'. Despite the President's concerns the event remained peaceful.

Reflecting on the march's impact in 2013, historian Nathan Connolly explained: 'The March on Washington helped create a new national understanding of the problems of racial and economic injustice'. Before the march many white Americans weren't engaged with civil rights issues. But afterwards, polls showed that racial injustice was seen as the country's number one concern.

The march was also successful in creating momentum for the 1964 Civil Rights Act, which addressed discrimination on the basis of race or sex; the desegregation of schools, parks, swimming pools and other public facilities; and removed restrictions around voter registration.

When young people speak, the world listens

One of the unique qualities young people can bring to activism is an ability to be heard. Fresh voices have a distinct ability to break through discourse, spin and entrenched agendas. They can reach the heart of issues and make people really engage with old conversations in new ways.

What younger activists might lack in direct experience they make up for with ingenious ways of thinking, working, getting attention and inspiring action. One of the spaces where this is most visible is the Fridays for Future school strikes being led by teen climate activist Greta Thunberg. Greta made global headlines at 15 years old when she first began spending Fridays protesting for climate action outside the Swedish parliament. She was hardly the first person to strike as a form of protest, but when she turned up with a simple sign that read 'School Strike for Climate', her age, the directness of her message and her clear outsider status drew public and media attention in just a few days.

'When the school strike first started, it was deemed really radical', remembers Dr Briony Towers, a research fellow at the School of Global, Urban and Social Studies at Melbourne's RMIT University whose work focuses on child-centred climate change adaptation. 'Adults never quite know what to do when children and young people step up and step outside the traditional structures or systems that they have for expressing their views.'

Greta knew that her age and inexperience weren't a disadvantage, but a secret weapon. An older activist in the same spot probably wouldn't have drawn such a curious and enthusiastic response from the press and public. But coming from someone so young, the tone of the message shifted, making it near impossible for the adults passing by to ignore her.

The reality is that while young people often feel like adults don't want to listen or take them seriously, they possess a singular moral authority. There's a lot of power in being a physical representation of the future. As Greta said at the 2019 UN Climate Summit: 'The eyes of all future generations are upon you. And if you choose to fail us, I say – we will never forgive you'.

No matter what our age, activism requires us to move beyond the right now, to consider how our actions today are shaping the world of tomorrow. And all of us can use our personal spaces to create change.

Change starts at home

Obviously, not everyone gets the chance to address the UN about the issues that matter to them. Commonly when people talk about activism, there is a focus on making as much noise and reaching as many people as possible. But often, the most powerful conversations happen in private. Bringing issues up at home can be a really fruitful way to engage the people around you in causes that matter.

Think about it like this: when most people face a topic they don't understand or don't want to deal with they turn off. They close the newspaper, change the channel or switch tabs. But studies have shown that hearing about an issue or cause from a child can help people overcome socio-ideological barriers and engage with the topic more fully. Parents who talk about climate change with their children report higher levels of concern over the issues than those who don't. Every conversation matters and has the potential to help another person take action in their own life.

 # EXPLAINER

Extinction Rebellion are reinventing resistance

In recent years, Extinction Rebellion have emerged as one of the world's most visible climate action groups. Describing themselves as an international 'non-violent civil disobedience activist movement', XR (as they're often known) stand apart from previous movements due to their belief that traditional protest methods haven't proven to be effective enough in spurring the rapid change we need to address the climate crisis. In place of the usual actions, they preach massive economic disruption. Most often this takes the form of 'die-ins', protests that block roads and bridges, and attempt to shut down large sections of major cities. As XR put it, 'Without economic cost the guys running this world really don't care.'

Through these die-ins, they also aim to force the citizens whose days are interrupted by the action to pause and think about the climate emergency and how much more severely their regular routines will be impacted if we don't act. XR has attracted considerable media attention for their commitment to these actions, with protesters often going as far as gluing or handcuffing themselves in place to avoid being removed by the police – and many participants willingly allow themselves to be arrested. However, the group stresses that their work and demands extend far beyond these dramatic events and they don't require participants to be willing to be arrested to become involved.

Ultimately, Extinction Rebellion has three main demands:

* The government must declare a climate emergency.
* The government must legally commit to reducing carbon emissions to net zero by 2025.
* A citizens' assembly must be formed to oversee the above changes. The assembly would be made up of a randomly selected group of people who represent a wide cross-section of society. They would consult with climate experts and stakeholders to 'deliberate on policy options and make recommendations that shape government responses'.

Extinction Rebellion hope to mobilise 3.5 per cent of the population – the figure reported to be needed to achieve social change – to persuade governments to commit to these demands.

Chapter Two

GET Connected

A generation online

It's impossible to talk about millennials' and gen Z's unique impact on activism in the 21st century without talking about the internet and social media. Nothing has had a bigger impact on the way we organise, communicate, create change or really do anything. It's difficult to imagine what movements like Black Lives Matter, Me Too or Occupy Wall Street would have looked like before smartphones.

Not only has technology transformed our causes, but it has also reshaped the role and individual impact of activists. With a phone in hand, anyone has the ability to educate, inform, expose and serve as a reporter, documentary maker or social organiser. Today you don't need an army to act, just a wi-fi connection.

Speed it up

As Dr Max Halupka, senior research fellow and theorist in digital politics from the University of Canberra, told Amnesty International: 'One thing that the internet has done is condensing time, space and identity.' There's no doubt that the biggest effect the internet and social media has had on activism is to speed it up. In the past, action took time. Like, a lot of time. Sometimes years or decades. But now, the right tweet can change the course of a situation overnight.

That's what happened in 2017 when President Donald Trump announced his hugely controversial order banning people from

 # ACTION

Strategic hashtags

We all know hashtags are a great way to find and share content around an issue. But when selecting which ones you use, think about who you want to communicate with.

Yes, by including hashtags tied to a specific cause, you're speaking to people who you know are interested and engaged in that work – but you can also be strategic to get your message into new spaces or in front of the people whose minds you're seeking to change. During the 2020 Black Lives Matter protests, many activists were encouraging the use of hashtags tied to pro-police and pro-Trump causes, in an effort to get their content into feeds that might not normally be flooded with this information.

Offer Alternatives

Decentralising yourself within an issue is about more than keeping your mouth shut. You need to also seek out ways to give up some of your space for others. One good place to start is in your professional life. If you have a website, or use platforms like Linkedin, consider how you could utilise that space to help others access employment opportunities. Your professional bio could include a section that directs people to those in your industry who have historically been disadvantaged or overlooked. If you're white, that could mean linking to Black, Indigenous and people of colour with similar skills to you, who could be considered in your place. Or if you're asked to speak at an event, you could politely decline and suggest someone else as an alternative.

# EXPLAINER

Occupy Wall Street
and the pros and cons of speed

Kicking off in New York in 2011, Occupy Wall Street began when a small group of protesters set up camp in Manhattan's Zuccotti Park. They were there to protest income inequality and the corrupting role of corporate money in politics. Their message and criticism of traditional keepers of financial power resonated with people around the world. Soon after images of the Occupy protest were shared online, hundreds of individuals set up demonstrations and campsites in their own cities' financial districts.

For the Occupy Wall Street movement, this sudden attention was a gift and a curse: the wide-reaching interest allowed it to grow fast, but that explosion meant that organisers didn't have much time to formulate a list of directions or demands. Being a leaderless movement, there were also internal structural challenges; leaders and supporters struggled to direct the ballooning support and attention into clear actions.

As a result, the Occupy Wall Street movement is often viewed as a failure. Eventually the attention dried up, people packed up their tents and the financial industry appeared to carry on largely unchanged. But almost a decade later, it's clear that this flash point did trigger wider change by introducing a language for ordinary people to express their frustration with wealth inequality. In the years after the protests fast-food workers in the United States walked off the job to protest the minimum wage. They were eventually successful in having it raised. Many of the issues tackled by Occupy have also dominated elections around the world, as ordinary citizens push politicians to grapple with the power of the economic one per cent.

several predominantly Muslim countries from entering the United States. The order was issued on a Friday, but rumours predicting it had been swirling around online for days. In response, the International Refugee Assistance Project had begun rallying lawyers, as they knew refugees who were already travelling to the United States when the ban came into effect were going to land and be stuck. The group's speed and use of social media meant that they were able to mobilise thousands of lawyers, who immediately headed out to offer assistance at airports across the country.

Social media has also let new voices emerge much faster than they ever could have in the past. Traditionally, political leaders tended to be older because it took a long time to work your way up to the job. Now we're seeing people like New York congresswoman Alexandria Ocasio-Cortez break through in just a few years. In 2018 AOC, as she's called, became the youngest woman ever elected to the US Congress. She was only 28 years old. A few years earlier she'd still been waiting tables. But her path to Congress was accelerated when her campaign video went viral, and her progressive ideas, wit, charm and impressive emoji skills made her a Twitter star.

Access all areas

Social media and the internet have democratised news and information by breaking down traditional hierarchies of who and what gets reported. In the past, the press were the gatekeepers of public information. When that worked it meant that responsible and committed journalists could champion individual voices and issues. But you still needed to get in front of the press to benefit from their attention. As a result, even the most progressive publications had a history of prioritising older, mostly white, often male voices.

I always feel the movement is a sort of MOSAIC. Each of us puts in *one little stone*, and then you get a great mosaic at the end

Alice Paul

But as Sarah J. Jackson, co-author of *#HashtagActivism: Networks of race and gender justice*, wrote in *The New York Times*: 'Many people who lacked public platforms 10 years ago – the young and members of marginalised groups in particular – are speaking up, insisting on being heard'. In her book she looks at how Twitter has allowed African Americans, survivors of gendered violence and transgender women to build communities and influence politics. Additionally, hashtags like #MeToo and #YesAllWomen have added countless voices to conversations that we may never have heard on the traditional news.

Bringing activism into the online space has also welcomed individuals who might have otherwise had issues accessing protests or meetings. Now if you can't make it down to a march or sit-in, you can still be part of the action by following developments on live streams or Twitter. This means that activists in regional areas or who have mobility limitations do not have to miss out.

How video can change the world

One of the most direct ways social media has changed activism is through the use of camera phones – especially with issues of police violence. Not only does the capture and distribution of videos force accountability for police actions, but it also brings them into the public sphere. Unfortunately, without video footage, the majority of complaints about police assaults never lead to convictions or repercussions.

Citizen camera people came into their own during the 2020 Black Lives Matter protests that were held across the United States (and the world). In his article in *New York Times* 'The Videos That Rocked America. The Song That Knows Our Rage', Wesley Morris wrote: 'The most urgent filmmaking anybody's doing in this country right now is by black people with camera phones'.

Protestors were able to hold biased media to account by sharing extended and unedited video that demonstrated how mainstream news outlets were manipulating footage of rallies. In one case, widely broadcast news footage showed NYPD cars slowly edging into a crowd to disrupt protesters. But a longer version of the clip saw one of the cars then speed up, putting members of the public in very real danger.

Real change still takes time

While social media and the internet are great for getting attention, starting conversations, reaching new audiences and accessing information, they can't sustain a movement on their own. In her book *Twitter and Tear Gas*, Turkish writer, academic and techno-sociologist Zeynep Tufekci explained that with speed comes weakness: 'The ease with which current social movements form often fails to signal an organising capacity powerful enough to threaten those in authority'.

When the Occupy Wall Street movement exploded in 2011, the internet helped the group's message opposing social and economic inequality to spread around the world within weeks. But while the movement grew at lightning-fast speed, it struggled to sustain itself or create change; organisers didn't have time to formulate a clear list of ideals, directions or demands. As a result, things eventually petered out and we don't talk as much about Occupy Wall Street today. Sometimes, it doesn't pay to move too fast.

To maintain an action for months, years or even decades you need more than a Facebook group. You need the support and trust of a solid community of like-minded activists, which is why the most impactful actions pair digital activism with traditional, person-to-person methods.

EXPLAINER

Black Lives Matter went from a Facebook post to a global movement

In 2012, Trayvon Martin, an unarmed 17-year-old African-American boy, was shot by neighbourhood watch volunteer George Zimmerman. Zimmerman claimed he acted in self-defence, following a confrontation with the teenager. He was charged with second-degree murder, but later acquitted.

Zimmerman's acquittal led to a national debate around civil rights and gun violence, and brought together three activists and community organisers who previously didn't know each other. Alicia Garza wrote a Facebook post called 'A Love Note to Black People' that included the phrase 'our lives matter, black lives matter'. In response, Patrisse Cullors replied with #BlackLivesMatter. Drawn to their message, Opal Tometi soon joined in, establishing a website and social media platforms to help people connect and to serve as the base of a new on-the-ground political network.

In 2014 #BlackLivesMatter went viral following the police killings of Eric Garner and Michael Brown. Again, no one was convicted, but the group emerged as a major activist force, committed to working to 'eradicate white supremacy and build local power to intervene in violence inflicted on Black communities by the state and vigilantes'. Black Lives Matter has since expanded to become a global network fighting state-sanctioned violence and anti-Black racism around the world.

Combining online and IRL

When groups manage to strike a balance of online and offline action, they can achieve incredible things. The Black Lives Matter and Me Too movements have both found ways to use online spaces to grow and enrich their causes, while creating real-world change. When the #BlackLivesMatter hashtag was first used in 2013 following the acquittal of George Zimmerman in the shooting death of Trayvon Martin, it immediately became a place where people from all over the world shared their anger, pain and frustration over the issue.

Five years later, the Pew Research Center found the hashtag was still being used on average 17,000 times a day. Its continued resilience, and the power of the movement, wasn't totally due to social media though. Over those years the Black Lives Matter movement grew and strengthened offline, with activists around the United States coming together with a shared, clear and powerful mission to disrupt the state-sanctioned violence inflicted on communities of colour.

The Me Too movement also shows how you can use social media to create a common language for an action and reach a huge audience while still maintaining roots in traditional activism. Tarana Burke founded the hashtag in 2006 as a way for survivors of sexual violence to share their experiences. Burke's activism and work with survivors extends way beyond Twitter, but in 2017 #MeToo became the collective online gathering space for people to speak out about sexual assault in Hollywood and other industries, demonstrating how social media can allow a diverse group of people to join the same conversation, as well as create room in movements for both self-expression and political participation.

Protest beyond the law is NOT a departure from DEMOCRACY; it is absolutely ESSENTIAL TO IT *

Howard Zinn

 # EXPLAINER

Tarana Burke and the rise of #MeToo

While the Me Too movement (and the seminal #MeToo hashtag) feels like a fairly recent social phenomenon, the group's work and impact stretches back to 2006. That's when activist Tarana Burke coined the phrase as a way to support women and girls of colour as they shared their experience of sexual violence.

Eleven years later, the term went viral after *The New York Times* published a bombshell investigation accusing media mogul Harvey Weinstein of a number of sexual assaults. That article kicked off waves of similar allegations against other powerful men, and inspired individuals around the world to speak out and share their own experiences on social media.

Actor Alyssa Milano tweeted: 'If you've been sexually harassed or assaulted write "me too" as a reply to this tweet.' The hashtag exploded, and Tarana Burke's desire to create a space for people to find a sense of solidarity went global. It didn't take long for the message to extend beyond Hollywood. In the months that followed accusations were levelled against athletic coaches, politicians, musicians, business tycoons and celebrity chefs, as well as countless non-celebrities.

A year later over 300 women working in Hollywood set up the anti-harassment coalition Time's Up. It included a legal defence fund to support individuals who had experienced harassment, assault or abuse in the workplace. The Time's Up coalition also called on movie studios and agencies to commit to a 50-50 gender balance of power within two years, and inspired countless other businesses and industries to do the same.

If they don't give you a *SEAT AT THE TABLE*, bring in a *FOLDING* CHAIR*

Shirley Chisholm

Chapter Three

HOW
to Find
Your
VOICE

What do you stand for?

Activism is a powerful thing. It has the ability to change communities and lives, and reorder the way we think about our place in the world. But it's also a lot of work. Any activist will tell you that engaging with a cause in a meaningful and sustainable way requires massive amounts of time and energy. Making sure that you don't burn out or disengage is an ongoing job, requiring you to constantly reflect on and evaluate your mission, approach, collaborators, and the way this work impacts your life and body (but more on that later).

The best way to make sure that you're able to stick with it for the long haul is to have a clear and deep understanding of what you're fighting for. At first this sounds easy: most people who take the time to head down to a protest or sign a petition know what they're getting into. But that understanding needs to extend beyond *what* you're doing, to *why* you're doing it.

Engaging with a cause that impacts or speaks to you is a lifelong process. It will require you to never stop educating yourself, questioning your own experiences, and pressing the people around you to be and do better. But if you take the time to really engage with the more personal and private parts of activism it can be an endlessly enriching journey. One that not only helps you create positive change, but also serves your mental health, introduces you to new people and helps you see the world you live in more clearly.

* The opposite of love is not hate, it's *INDIFFERENCE*. The opposite of art is not ugliness, it's **INDIFFERENCE**. The opposite of faith is not heresy, it's *INDIFFERENCE*. And the opposite of life is not death, it's INDIFFERENCE

Elie Wiesel

 # ACTION

Start a book club

Reading is a great way to explore the history, voices and philosophy of your cause. But it can sometimes feel overwhelming to sit down and tackle a pile of literature on your own. A book club is a nice way to make the task seem more manageable, and discussing what you learn with other people will help you absorb and build on new ideas.

Commit to reading one chapter at a time, then come together and discuss. You can prepare questions or talking points if you like, or just let people share how they're feeling about the text. This is not only a good way to educate yourself, it can also be a fun opportunity to get to know activists in your community and even engage friends with your cause. If you need a bit of help choosing what books to feature, ask other organisers you know about the books that inspire and drive them. Or look up what your favourite writers, thinkers and cultural leaders are reading and loving.

The power of a clear message

Whether you're working alone or as part of a group, it's important to consider what values and beliefs drive your work. This doesn't need to be a hugely complex process. It's not about sitting down on day one and executing a flawless plan detailing what the rest of your life as an activist will look like. The goal here is to come up with a clear and direct message that reflects what you stand for, what you want and how others can take part.

Knowing your values will help you stay focused on the bigger picture and not become overwhelmed by an endless list of things you *could* be doing. If you're working within a group, or starting an action that will invite others to take part, establishing a set of values is a way to efficiently and clearly communicate your central purpose. Keeping your values broad helps other individuals to engage with them and allows everyone to find themselves within the cause.

Building community through activism

Like a lot of things, activism is best enjoyed with friends. A support network will help you refine your values, educate yourself and others, celebrate victories and offer encouragement when things get tough. With the internet it's easy to connect with like-minded activists, but in-person friendships are especially valuable and nourishing.

That's not to say that you can't turn a Twitter pal into an IRL connection. If there is someone you admire in your area, consider asking if they'd like to catch up and chat in person. Just be careful; even within an activist community you should always play it safe.

Try to only meet with people with whom you share mutual friends, always do so in a public place and take a buddy along the first few times. No matter how much you enjoy someone's online presence, it doesn't mean you should ever go to their house or somewhere else isolated until you really know them in the flesh. If even meeting in public seems a bit overwhelming, you could suggest a phone call instead. Activists are busy people, so a catch-up buzz during a lunch break might be a better option.

Also, don't discount the people around you. Just because your friends and family don't seem as motivated as you are right now doesn't mean you can't get them there. Talk to them about why this cause matters to you; make it personal. It's easier for people to connect with an issue when they see how it impacts those they care about. It also might encourage them to think about how it touches their own lives.

Start small with simple acts of engagement: give them a book you love, invite them to a talk or watch a movie that deals with themes you've been wrestling with. Remember, the start of your activist journey is an easy entry point for other people to join you. You can all figure things out together. Community connections (aka friends) have proven to be one of the key factors in building resilient movements and keeping people engaged in their work. Because of this, successful movements often focus on scaling out, not *up*. That means rather than trying to make the whole world listen right away, you start with the people around you, bringing them to your cause and then encouraging them to spread the message in their own communities. That kind of person-to-person connection will go a lot further towards changing attitudes than shouting at someone on the internet.

One child,
one teacher,
one book and
one pen can
CHANGE THE
WORLD*

Malala Yousafzai

Prioritising diversity and learning to listen

At the beginning of this process, while you're thinking about your values and the people you engage with, it's important to take a moment to reflect on the power and importance of diversity in any movement. Diversity is one of those words that gets thrown around a lot and can mean a lot of things. Here, at its most basic, it's about inviting in, listening to and taking feedback from people who have experiences that are different from yours.

Sometimes in activism making space for all kinds of people means giving up some of your own. The most direct way of committing to diversity is really listening to the people around you, not just waiting for your chance to talk or hoping they'll say something you already agree with. As activists, we need to be conscious of creating environments where everyone feels safe to share not only their experiences, but also their feedback.

Listening to and reflecting on criticism is one of those things we all say we're willing to do, until asked to actually do it. It's not easy when someone presses back on your values, ideas or work. But those (admittedly) painful experiences are vital in growing as an individual and building a movement. It's often harder to give feedback than receive it. So be respectful of the energy and vulnerability the other person is offering you. Thank them for taking the time to speak with you and ensure you don't just listen, but also act.

Many worthy causes have been felled by infighting, division and accusations of exclusivity. So making sure a culture of openness is central to your activism will only make your work and community stronger in the long term.

 # ACTION

Look up your neighbourhood's Indigenous history and Pay the Rent

For all the time we spend in our neighbourhoods, getting to know the area, some of us forget to consider the Indigenous history of where we live. There are many resources online that lay out the background of specific areas around the world, and even provide apps or walking tours to help you become better acquainted with significant historic landmarks.

Spend an afternoon reading up about where you live, and visit any important sights nearby. But don't stop there: make an effort to share what you learn with your friends and neighbours.

Once you have a better understanding of the history of where you live, consider Paying the Rent. In Australia, this refers to the longstanding calls from Indigenous activists for people to donate money to Traditional Owners for the occupation of land they live on.

If you're not in a position to make a monetary donation, consider how you could dedicate your time supporting First Nations causes.

Unity in difference

Many of the world's largest and most successful movements find strength in the understanding that while our individual causes might be different, the fight for a truly safer, fairer, cleaner, more sustainable future is a unified one. As Martin Luther King Jr famously wrote in his 'Letter from a Birmingham Jail': 'Injustice anywhere is a threat to justice everywhere. We are caught in an inescapable network of mutuality, tied in a single garment of destiny. Whatever affects one directly, affects all indirectly.'

Whether you're passionate about supporting the rights of people of colour, refugees, LGBTQIA+ individuals, animals, students or any other impacted group, you're fighting against the same systems of power, greed and oppression. When they recognise who they're working against, activist groups can support and inspire each other across causes.

In 2017 millions of women from all around the world took part in the Women's March. Attendance numbers were so large, and the cause was picked up in so many cities, it's widely believed to be impossible to estimate the total number of participants. At the time, it was reported to have been the largest protest in US history.

The march was officially organised to protest the election of Donald Trump. But those huge numbers were possible because countless individuals worldwide were able to align their personal causes with the stand against the new US president. The crowds were made up of people marching for the rights of women, but also for migrants, queer communities, people of colour, family violence survivors and many others. By recognising a shared cause and adversary, these groups were able to come together and make history.

When immersing yourself in research, take time to pause and ask: who else is impacted by this issue? If a system of power is

 # ACTION

Suggest a phone call

Look around you (or at your online community) and identify someone who you really look up to and admire. Maybe it's a writer, journalist, academic, organiser or even an acquaintance you respect. Ask if they'd be interested in having a phone or video call to discuss their work. People are busy, so keep the chat focused and succinct. Consider preparing a few questions or talking points ahead of time, and let them know when you reach out what you're specifically interested in. While there's nothing wrong with abandoning your notes if the conversation begins to flow freely, coming prepared shows you respect them and their time. Once you get over the initial nerves of meeting a stranger, try to make a habit of it. Set a personal goal of speaking to one interesting new person a month.

When immersing yourself in research, take time to pause and ask: who else is impacted by this issue? If a system of power is oppressive to you, chances are it's oppressive to others. Review your work and your values to consider how you can engage with individuals outside of your immediate circle. Maybe that means reading a book about an aligned cause, attending a meeting run related to one of their projects, or even reevaluating your work as a whole to more meaningfully include topics related to their agenda.

 **ACTION**

Create a set of values

Take the time to create a set of values, either for yourself or your group. This can be a useful tool to help guide, focus and motivate your efforts. If you're working on it alone, think about what drives you. Imagine looking at this list in a day and in a decade, to consider what these values will mean across time.

Creating a set of values for a group is a bit more of a complex process; you need to ensure everyone is able to contribute and share what matters to them. Invite people to bring their own suggestions and discuss them together. Start with a longer list of possible core values, and refine it over time. Don't rush. This can take years to get right. It's ok to tweak and change things as you go. Keep group values relatively broad, simple and relatable. You want to make sure anyone can look at them and feel they apply to their life and work.

While there is no magic number, it can be worth keeping the number of values limited. Start by trying to come up with five.

oppressive to you, chances are it's oppressive to others. Review your work and your values to consider how you can engage with individuals outside of your immediate circle. Maybe that means reading a book about an aligned cause, attending a meeting related to one of their projects, or even re-evaluating your work as a whole to more meaningfully include topics to their agenda.

Finding a mentor

Just as important as unity in activism, is experience. Sometimes the easiest way to learn is to talk to people who have been there and done that. That's why mentors are so valuable. They can offer support, answer questions, motivate, connect and point you in the direction of other valuable and trusted resources. But finding a mentor can be a daunting task.

One of the simplest ways to meet more experienced activists is to engage with existing groups. That doesn't mean you need to sideline your personal projects. Rather, look for organisations that share your values and reach out to see if you can be involved.

Sometimes participating in an existing group can help you get a sense of what works, what doesn't, what you find inspiring and what you'd like to try to improve on. Collaborating with established groups can also open up networks of people and resources that can take a long time to crack on your own.

Don't be shy. Introduce yourself to people or ask for introductions, suggest a coffee or even a phone call (people are busy).

It's important to remember that not everyone will have the ability to commit to mentorship in the ways you want. The person you approach might already have a group of fresh activists they're working with, or their other life commitments could make it tricky for them to take on more responsibility. If that's the case, don't be discouraged. It might take a few tries to find the right person.

 **EXPLAINER**

The Women's March

On 21 January 2017, women around the world gathered together for a series of marches that stretched from New York to Sydney. The protests took place the day after the inaugural parade of President Donald Trump: throughout the 2016 US presidential campaign, Trump had been dogged by allegations of sexual harassment against multiple women. The decision to gather together was seen as an act of resistance against the newly elected president. But what started as a stand against Trump quickly evolved into a much larger call to interrogate the rights of women around the world, and an expression of female rage and frustration.

The iconic Women's March began with one woman and a single act of defiance. The day after Trump's election in December 2016, a Hawaii-based grandmother called Teresa Shook expressed her frustration on Facebook, suggesting to forty of her friends that they march in Washington DC. Her message was shared wider than she could ever have expected. Soon, thousands of women were pledging to join her and take a stand. The sentiment spread around the world, engaging millions of people and inspiring the organisation of hundreds of similar events.

These separate actions were eventually brought together as the official Women's March on Washington. Although final numbers are difficult to estimate, especially on a global scale, it's believed millions of women gathered in Washington for that first event, making it one of the largest single-day protests in US history.

In the years since, people have continued to gather annually to fight for the rights of women everywhere. The Women's March is unique in its broad message and reach, calling for women to attend and stand for issues that personally impact them. More recently, the group's platform has also put specific focus on immigration reform, climate justice and reproductive justice.

As with Occupy Wall Street, organisers have faced criticism over their seeming inability to channel the huge participation numbers into political actions. But academics have noted that the Women's March events appear to have served a different purpose. Dana R. Fisher, Professor of Sociology at the University of Maryland, has looked at the experiences of people who attended the Women's March. She noted that 'a third of the people who were there had no experience with protester activism before. But they went back to their communities, and in many cases joined social movement organisations or political movement organisations, and then ended up getting involved in a whole bunch of activities around the elections in 2018'. This would suggest that the Women's March has had a long-term impact as an engagement point for a new generation of activists.

Delving deeper

There is no perfect movement, no flawless activist and no unbeatable argument. A lot of this work is about facing up to what you *don't* know, being humble enough to ask for help and patient enough to educate yourself. While friends and mentors are vital, it's also important to be willing to put in the work alone. Striving for social change can be exhausting, and you can't always rely on other people to explain everything to you.

If you're not sure where to begin, educate yourself! Go back and research the history of your movement or the cause you're passionate about. Understand how it has impacted groups over generations, learn the names of people who went before you, consider the work they did and where they found success. If possible, read their writing and reflections, or seek out interviews with them. Understanding the history of a movement also helps you keep your ego in check. Remember that this issue didn't begin when you discovered it.

Also consider how the causes you're interested in may impact Indigenous communities. First Nations people are often among the earliest groups affected by issues such as climate change. Take the time to listen, and research what they're already fighting for. Maybe your voice is best used in support of theirs.

Reader beware

Luckily, when it comes to educating yourself, there are endless resources to help you out. But while we're spoiled for choice in books, articles, podcasts and documentaries, it's important to remember that we're living in an age of misinformation. The internet has allowed a lot of opinions to spread, and not all of them are reputable or constructive. So make sure you're consulting trustworthy resources.

Here are a few steps to help you determine if a source is reliable:

* **Start with yourself and your own biases.** It's human nature to seek out information that confirms what you already believe and feel. Always ask yourself: do I believe this because I want it to be true, or because it's *truly* trustworthy?

* **Check the author and sources.** Look up other work by this person and try to spot if they have an agenda. Have they worked for companies that could be impacted by the issues they're discussing? Do they work with reputable agencies? Are they quoting networks, periodicals and other sources that feel legitimate or are authorities on these topics? Also, watch out for paid articles or pieces from think tanks that might have a political agenda. They're easy to mistake for regular news reporting.

* **Read the whole article.** Headlines and even opening paragraphs can be sensationalist and misleading. Always make it to the end of a document before forming an opinion on it.

* **Check the date.** A lot can change in a few days or hours. When it comes to news always look for the most recent reputable offering.

* **Fact-check it yourself.** You don't need a huge amount of knowledge of an issue to perform basic fact-checking. Start by trying to confirm any specific data, quotes and figures across multiple news sources. If the piece you're reading differs massively from the wider reporting it might be worth disregarding. A fake quote or statistic will bring up other articles flagging it as false.

* **Use reverse image search.** Fake news sites or shady publications will sometimes misuse images to give a false sense of a story. But a reverse Google search can show where an image originated, what it's of and what other people are saying about it. All this additional information will help you make up your own mind about whether it was correctly used.

* **View footage and photos from multiple angles.** Unfortunately, you can't always trust what you see. Not only can photos be doctored, but editing, framing and camera perspectives can be used to tell different stories. If you find a photo or video that feels important, see if you can contrast and compare it to other images or footage.

* **Know the difference between news and opinion.** News and opinion are both valuable in understanding an issue, but it's not always easy to separate what someone feels from the facts. News should always be reported straight: just an account of what happened, without any personal perspective or comments.

* **If it's a website, read the 'About Us' section.** Even if it's brief, this will usually give you a sense of who works there, who runs it and what their values are. Ask yourself if it feels like these people are impartial and trustworthy. Trust your gut. If this section reads weirdly, or seems overly dramatic or unprofessional, find another source.

* **Watch out for satire.** Sometimes people are tripped up by an article or post that's misleading or ridiculous on purpose. It pays to research the publication, look at other content from the same publisher and read their About Us section.

 **EXPLAINER**

How the Parkland students inspired Greta Thunberg

When Greta Thunberg took a seat outside the Swedish parliament in August 2018, she couldn't have known that her simple action would go on to inspire millions of other school children around the world to eventually stage their own strikes for climate change. Ironically, at the time, she was herself following the lead of activists she admired. Earlier in the year, she'd paid close attention to the news of the Parkland school shooting in Florida and the resulting protests by the student body.

Greta was particularly moved by how these students were able to inspire their peers. Following the tragedy, young people across the United States joined the Parkland survivors to stage a series of school walkouts protesting their country's gun laws and culture – taking action over an issue that the grown-ups around them had seemingly stalled on. When politicians and other adults revealed that they weren't the leaders that the community needed, the Parkland students demonstrated that they were able to take over and eventually formed the March for Our Lives movement.

In turn, Parkland student organiser Emma González has come to equally respect Greta. Writing about her in *Time* magazine she said, 'Greta Thunberg saw her power in us, and we in turn see our power in her.'

# ACTION

Think beyond your own physical experience

Diversity doesn't just relate to how we look or think, but also how we experience the world. If you're organising a meeting or action, make sure to ask yourself: is this space accessible and available to everyone? What are the obstacles that could block someone from participating and feeling welcome here?

Some adjustments you could make include bringing in a sign language interpreter, changing the location to ensure it's wheelchair accessible or near public transport, organising a carpool for people without transport or live streaming the event.

Question time

Whether you're new to a group, just starting to engage with a mentor figure or have been working in these spaces for decades, it always pays to ask questions. Chances are, if something is unclear or confusing to you, it probably is for other people too. Speaking up in a group allows everyone to get more clarity on a topic. Also, asking for further explanation or more context can gently let the other person know they might need to adjust their communication style.

Asking questions is especially vital when so many of us are still learning how to differentiate between trusted and malicious information online. Chatting to people around you can offer much-needed clarity on topics you might be learning about alone.

On the other side of things, try to never make anyone feel awkward for asking a question. Even if it seems simplistic or obvious to you, it shows they care and are trying to learn more. You have to respect that effort.

 # ACTION

Talk to someone who is sharing fake news

As you're learning to be aware of fake or misleading news, you may start to notice more people around you sharing it. While it's important to disrupt the spread of misinformation, it can be a bit awkward to call out someone who thinks they're engaging with a legitimate source (especially when it confirms their own point of view).

If you see someone sharing content you think is misleading, encourage them to review the piece themselves following the steps outlined in this chapter. Where possible, intervene privately and be sensitive. The goal is to help them learn how to spot problematic reporting so they can be more careful in the future, without making them feel embarrassed or attacked.

This is a chance to help them become more careful online – not a chance to lecture or try to force your own opinion on them. Consider sharing some resources or trusted sites that you have found helpful, and explain why you believe they're worthwhile.

Sometimes, if someone is making problematic claims or sharing dangerous information publicly (say, on Facebook or Twitter), you may need to be more direct. Try to be civil and remember they're also just trying to understand the world around them. Blowing up and losing your cool isn't going to help anyone see things your way.

 **EXPLAINER**

How to use hand signals in a meeting

Organising actions and running meetings is vital work, but managing a room full of people has its challenges. Even the most prepared person can find it a bit chaotic at times. When everyone wants to have their say, things can quickly dissolve into a noisy muddle of voices and opinions. One way to keep things on track is to employ hand signals for people to use during discussions. This helps conversations stay on track, avoids too many disruptions and makes it easier for quieter participants to be heard. Rather than shouting out when you have something to say, use one of these signals:

* **Raising your hand:** I would like to say something.

* **Pointing a finger:** I have a direct response to what's been said.

* **Holding the front of your hands up:** I agree.

* **Holding the back of your hands up:** I disagree.

* **Making your hand into a C shape:** I need you to clarify

* **Finger pointed up:** Please speak louder.

There are many, many more signals you can use. Look them up online and make a guide you can print out or share at your next meeting.

Chapter Four

ACTIVISM
in
Action:
PROTESTS

Why we protest

When most of us think about activism, we probably picture people taking to the streets to protest. Across countries, generations and causes, street protests have become one of the most iconic and popular ways to take a stand. Throughout history street protests have been responsible for transforming geopolitics, forcing the resignation of politicians and toppling authoritarian governments. But not only do they draw attention to an issue, they also create bonds between activists and foster a greater sense of solidarity.

Academics have spent decades studying protests to understand what exactly makes them successful. Erica Chenoweth, a political scientist at Harvard University, has been central in this work. In her 2013 TEDx talk 'The Success of Nonviolent Civil Resistance' she introduced the theory that for a social movement to bring about a real shift, it only needs to meaningfully engage 3.5 per cent of the general population. To reach that figure she studied over a century of social movements, and found that no group who hit that threshold failed to bring about change.

In recent years, our relationship to protests has evolved as they've become more common. And while COVID-19 highlighted other forms of activism, there is no doubt they will always be central to actions.

Most of us attending protests aren't out to overthrow the government. Rather, we show up to express how we feel to policymakers and people in positions of power. In that way, protests are vital spaces to begin engaging with causes. In fact, attending a protest is the first action of many new activists.

ACTIVISM WORKS. So what I'm telling you to do now, is to act. Because *no one is too small* to make a difference *

Greta Thunberg

That being said, the impact of physical street protests on politics and public opinion is real and observable. Princeton political science professor Omar Wasow has researched how protests influence voting behaviour and patterns in the US. Across his work he found that communities that were exposed to nonviolent protest activity were more likely to vote liberally in presidential elections. But those that were exposed to violent events were more likely to vote conservatively.

Power in numbers

Protests offer opportunities to strengthen a sense of mutual support and unity within activist culture. As we've mentioned, constantly fighting for what you believe in can get tiring. So it's important to find spaces where people can be reinvigorated, reinspired or even discover a movement.

Being, by design, such open and public events, protests are also an easy way to access new ideas and actions. You don't need to be an official member of a group or possess any sophisticated knowledge to join a march. That's especially valuable for kids and teens, who are unable to engage in many other parts of political discourse, like voting. Public protests give younger activists a chance to be seen and heard, and encourage a sense of agency.

That momentum isn't left behind when people pack up their banners and signs for the day. As demonstrated at the 2017 Women's March, protests have been shown to drive ongoing, deeper engagement with activist work among attendees.

# ACTION

Be conscious of your content

As mentioned, protests are highly public places. Just because you're comfortable to share photos of yourself doesn't mean everyone else is. The sensitivities around sharing pictures and videos online can't be stressed enough. You never want to compromise the security and privacy of people around you.

Simply altering or blurring an image in Photoshop isn't enough. Also use stickers, emojis and other editing tools to make sure people can't be identified. When you're ready to post, screenshot the image and share that version, not the original. Photos taken on your phone are embedded with metadata that could include locations and private information. Finally, if you're not able to edit your videos to protect people's identities, don't post them.

Give peace a chance

Research has shown that for a protest to be successful, it doesn't only need to reach 3.5 per cent of the population. It should also remain peaceful. Considering that these events are often the first time people might hear about a cause, it's important to make a good impression. All protests are in some ways trying to disrupt people's everyday lives and force them to literally face an issue. But while violence may draw attention, it also creates chaos and distrust, which poisons any chance of bringing about progressive, stable change. As previously mentioned, it can impact on how observers vote in the future, too. Erica Chenoweth's research also found that nonviolent protests are twice as likely to succeed as violent ones. So keep your cool.

That holds for evaluating protests too: while most activists encourage nonviolent actions, it's important to not jump to judgements when events get out of hand. Just because violence breaks out, it doesn't mean that the people involved have specifically chosen chaos over cooperation. In many cases people turn to violence or vandalism when they feel that other avenues of communication have failed or been ignored. When the 2020 Black Lives Matter protests at times turned violent, critics argued that participants were hurting their cause and suggested that they would see more success if they peacefully worked with law enforcement and government officials. Organisers pointed out that they'd been trying to work in these spaces for generations, but were still facing a reality where (often unarmed) people of colour were routinely being killed by police.

In her article 'Why People Loot' in *The Atlantic*, Olga Khazan said of the 2020 Black Lives Matter protests, '...some of the looting is a lashing-out against capitalism, the police, and other forces that are seen as perpetuating racism'. She also quoted a looter during the 1992 Los Angeles riots, who had told the Miami Herald: 'I don't think it's right, but it gets the frustrations out'.

How to protest like a pro

We have seen that protests are powerful, transformative events that can change minds, governments and countries. But they're also complicated undertakings and as such require a bit of planning for safe participation. So before you rush out to the next one, take the time to ensure you're ready to make the most of the day and the momentum it inspires.

One great way to do this is to see if you can get a group together. Not only will attending a protest with a group of mates make the whole experience more enjoyable, it can also be an important way to ensure you all remain safe throughout the day. If you do all end up heading in together, spend some time getting organised together too.

Stand out

A protest isn't a protest without a good sign (or even a homemade slogan tee). Set aside some time before the event to plan and design yours – with your friends if possible. The best signs are bright, clear and simple. Make sure your sign is legible from across the street, and check with organisers to see if there are any phrases or messages they're focusing on. This can help project a sense of unity, focus and teamwork within your movement.

Now a clever sign might get you on the news or even help you go viral on social media, but don't get too fixated on being overly clever. You want to make sure that it can be understood at a glance. No one is going to have time to stand there deciphering your jokes

*A change is brought about because **ORDINARY** people do **EXTRAORDINARY** things

Barack Obama

in the middle of a march. Although, if you are trying to build a following, remember to include your social media handle. If you do end up going viral you may as well get the credit.

Don't lose sight of what matters: signs are a way to tell everyone why you showed up and what inspires you. They also offer insights into other people's relationships with the cause. So remember to pause and appreciate all the great artwork around you, and reflect on how this event is impacting everyone differently.

Finally, consider making a few spares to hand out when you're there. This can be a nice way to start conversations with other protesters who might not be as prepared as you. If you see a member of the public taking a special interest in what's going on, you can offer them one of your extras to invite them into the action. Obviously don't push anyone who's not up for it, just let them know they're welcome.

Know your rights

Let's get serious for a minute. Protests are powerful, emotional events. So you should be ready in case things get tense. Laws and rights surrounding protests will differ depending on where you live, so do your research before you go to know what to do if things go awry.

A Google search can provide a good basic guide to the laws in your area, but you can also reach out to organisers to get a better understanding of what to expect on the day. If you are researching online, make sure you trust the source. Stick to government sites, mainstream news publications and established human rights groups. Double-check the source is speaking about your state or territory, so you are getting the right information.

There are a few things to keep in mind, no matter where you live: if you're stopped by the police, stay calm, be polite, keep your hands visible, and don't try to run away or antagonise them. Don't, under any circumstances, lie to a police officer.

Different countries and areas have different laws about answering police questions and giving your name. So do some research to find out what the police are allowed to ask you and your rights in regard to answering them.

To help you remember all your research, make a 'bust card'. This is a piece of paper that details your legal rights, in case you do have a confrontation with police. In the moment, it's easy to get overwhelmed so it's handy to have some basic steps to follow. Keep your bust card simple and straightforward. It may include a phone number of a lawyer or other emergency contact.

Pack wisely

Protests can involve a lot of standing, walking and waiting. They also tend to go for several hours so a bit of preparation can go a long way in making sure the whole experience isn't totally exhausting. Keep this checklist on hand when you're getting ready to make sure you have everything you need.

* **Comfy shoes:** You don't want to ruin your day with sore feet.

* **A hat and sunscreen:** Trust us, this isn't the time to get burnt.

* **Your phone and a charger (preferably portable):** If you're planning on filming, streaming and posting on social media over the course of the day your battery will go flat faster than usual.

* **A water bottle:** It's important to drink up. Even in cool weather you can easily become dehydrated.

* **Identification, bust card and emergency contact information:** Consider writing your emergency contact's name on your arm in case you lose your phone.

- **Energy snacks or bars:** Opt for something that will give you a boost without weighing you down.

- **Enough cash to get you home:** Make sure to keep it separate from your wallet – again, in case you lose it.

- **A watch:** You want to be prepared if your phone is out of action.

- **Pen and paper:** There is often a line-up of great speakers at protests and you might want to take notes.

- **A first aid kit:** Pack some wet wipes, tissues and bandaids. If you need medication like an inhaler, EpiPen or insulin make sure you have that too.

- **Offline messaging:** Consider downloading an app like FireChat that allows you to message your friends without signal or mobile data.

Final considerations

Think about your answers: Protests get a lot of attention, so be prepared for questions about what you're up to. It's even worth asking yourself: Am I the best person to answer? If passers-by want to hear more about the event, it can be a good chance to chat to new people about your cause. They may want to know why you are protesting and what you want to change. People might also be a bit peeved about being delayed or disturbed on their way to work or school, so consider what you could say to someone who is feeling frustrated to express how important this action is to you.

But if you're approached by the media, or asked to give a statement in a more formal context, pause before you say anything. Your off-the-cuff comment could be used to speak for everyone in attendance. Depending on the action, and your role within it, it might not be responsible or appropriate for you to take on the job of spokesperson.

Plan how you'll get home: A large protest could disrupt public transport and traffic. If possible, walk or ride your bike. If someone's picking you up, organise a meeting spot that's a little removed from the action. It will make it easier for you to find each other at the end of the day. Remember, your phone may not be working, so ensure your plans are concrete before you set out and they don't expect to hear from you to confirm.

Prepare mentally: While most people go to protests aiming for a peaceful and productive event, attending any direct action requires you to understand that things can take a turn for the worse. It's important to mentally prepare for that and discuss with your group how you would deal with it (more on that in a moment).

And one more time, charge your phone!

Look after each other (and yourself)

Before you leave home, make sure a friend or parent knows where you're going and roughly what time you'll be back. (And don't forget to check in with them when you're all done so they know you're ok.) Make sure you have emergency contact details for anyone you are going with too.

If you film or take photos of the protest do NOT include people's faces. If you can't avoid this, edit your images to obscure them (unless you have permission to post). Everyone is attending for different reasons; some people might not be open about their beliefs at home or work and you posting pictures of them could make life difficult or even dangerous.

This can all be a lot to stay across. If you are going with friends you can make things more manageable by assigning roles

 # ACTION

Save a packing list on your phone

While protests can vary greatly in terms of subject, crowd and mission, the basic requirements of what you need to pack tend to stay the same. When you have some free time, create an ultimate packing checklist that you can keep on your phone to help you get organised in the future. Doing this on a quiet afternoon (rather than just before an action) gives you space to think about what you really need and how much you're willing to carry. Once you've edited it all down to a final list, getting ready for any future actions will be a breeze.

Host a sign-making workshop

Different protests often call for specific messaging. But if you're consistently involved in a cause, you can easily reuse and pre-prepare signs and banners. Before a protest, invite some friends over to plan, design and create together. Working with other people often helps you feel more creative – you can bounce ideas around and give each other feedback.

By breaking out a chunk of time to do this, you can also create some spare signs to hand out at the event or keep on hand for next time. Remember to take care of your work so you can reuse it again and again. There's nothing sadder than seeing all the public bins stuffed with signs after an event.

It is not always the same thing to be a good MAN and a good CITIZEN *

Aristotle

within your group. Each person can be in charge of a specific responsibility: mental health, first aid, media liaison (if you all feel this is appropriate and someone wants to interview you), engaging with police or even just carrying snacks.

After the protest

Things don't end when everyone goes home. Remember, the real impact of a protest is how it mobilises people into ongoing actions. Take that buzzing energy and put it towards your next project.

Don't be shy about sharing your enthusiasm with others: post about the day on social media, talk to your friends and family, and share photos (if you have permission or have obscured people's identities). Check if there is a hashtag people are posting under to make your content more visible. Tell others how you feel, why the day mattered and what you hope comes next. Your enthusiasm will be infectious.

Once you've done that, consider emailing the organisers to ask how you could get involved in future events or support their cause between actions. Keep that momentum going. Talk to your friends about local community projects you could start together, reach out to established groups you'd like to support, or flip through this book and find an action to start today.

# ACTION

Form a protest crew

If you're attending protests regularly, it can be really nice to have a set group of friends who you head along with. By building an organised collective, you can share some of the responsibilities and pressure that demonstrations can invite.

Assign roles between you, deciding who will be responsible for what on the day. This allows you to focus on one thing well, instead of having to try to remember a pile of information. One way to break up responsibilities is: supplies, first aid, talking to the press and dealing with police. But don't limit yourself to that list; you know better than anyone what you need to feel safe and have a good time. Some of the more complex tasks, such as looking up specific protest rights and laws in your area, can often be more enjoyable to do with other people. It can also be worth sharing emergency contact details before you head out and talking about any medical conditions that others should be aware of.

Set ongoing goals

Hold yourself accountable for how you're going to stay engaged with a cause after the crowds, media coverage and social content disperse. The day after an action, sit down and make a list of things you want to incorporate into your life. Maybe it's reading a text related to this issue every month, setting up a direct debit to make a regular contribution to a cause, organising to volunteer your time or dedicating part of your week to pro-bono work. Be serious about these goals. Put them in your calendar and set a reminder to review them in a few months.

I am no longer
ACCEPTING the
things I cannot
change. I am
CHANGING *
the things I
cannot accept

Angela Davis

Chapter Five

THERE'S MORE *than One* Way to Take A STAND

Beyond the protest

As we mentioned in the previous chapter, taking to the streets is a powerful form of activism – but it's hardly the only one. For a campaign to be successful it needs more commitment than just a day out holding a sign. When the protest is over, it's time to figure out how you're going to take the cause home with you by dedicating yourself to sustained resistance in your own life. That means building a collection of actions that you feel you can keep engaging with on a daily, weekly, monthly and even yearly basis.

This broader, long-term approach to social change takes more work, but it's also been proven to be deeply effective. Abhinav Gupta is an assistant professor of strategic management at the University of Washington Foster School of Business who has researched the effectiveness of activist efforts. Across his work he has found that while protests can lead to immediate and localised success, long-term change needs 'evidence-based education efforts'. In short: it's important to keep learning, find ways to keep chatting to the people around us, and show our friends and family how these big issues relate to their daily lives too.

The easiest way to do that is to make activism a part of our routine, as regular as brushing our teeth. That allows us to be constantly (and naturally) engaging with causes while also bringing them to the attention of people around us. The reality is, this is where the real work, and impact, of personal activism lies. It also lets us send a powerful message that we're serious, and won't be discouraged or ignored. Our demands aren't going away – they're guiding and informing every decision we make. So people better get ready to listen.

* **EVERYONE thinks of changing the world but NO ONE thinks of changing himself**

Leo Tolstoy

 **EXPLAINER**

The Ice Bucket Challenge was here for a good time, not a long time

While a movement can't survive online alone, and we need to seek out ways to drive engagement for ongoing effectiveness, sometimes it's enough to just hold the public's attention for a moment. When the Ice Bucket Challenge went viral in 2014, founders Pat Quinn and Pete Frates were hoping to raise money and awareness for people living with motor neurone disease. The action was simple: they asked people to film themselves dumping a bucket of ice water on their head and then nominate someone else to do the same. If you wanted to opt out of the uncomfortable challenge you could choose to make a monetary donation to groups researching the disease instead. Despite seemingly dominating the whole internet for a few weeks, the trend eventually disappeared from public view. But that flash of attention was all Pat and Pete needed to have an impact.

During the month or so that the challenge was part of the zeitgeist, it's estimated that the campaign raised over $100 million that funded new research and led to breakthroughs in treating the disease.

Everyday activism

Keeping this spirit going requires multiple forms of everyday activism. These are the small ways we incorporate our values into everything we do. Remember, everything you eat, wear and buy sends a message. How you choose to spend your time and money casts a vote about the world you want to live in. Look around you, and think about the habits you can form and change to make sure you're living up to your values every day.

This day-to-day activism isn't only powerful, but it can also be enriching. By seeking out a diverse range of actions we make activist culture more accessible and welcoming. Many forms of direct action can be exclusionary for people in regional areas, or those who have mobility issues, are immunocompromised or aren't comfortable around large groups. But everyday activism can work for anyone. Boycotts, campaigns, petitions and digital projects have very few barriers to getting involved. You don't even need to put your shoes on to get to work.

Consumer activism

Consumer activism is arguably the easiest way to commit to social change each day because it's often less about what you do than what you don't do. It is built on the idea that the fastest way to get someone's attention is through their wallet. Most frequently taking the form of boycotts and 'buycotts', consumer activist actions encourage people not to support the business interests of organisations or individuals who are working in opposition to their cause. For example, if you're against the over-reliance on fossil fuels, you wouldn't put your money in a bank that invests in them.

The reasoning behind boycotts is simple: if you can't inspire someone or some business to do the right thing for social or political reasons, maybe you can motivate them for financial ones. If they believe that their behaviour is making them less desirable to consumers, they may change it. Sure, it's not quite as satisfying as waking them up to the broader issues, but someone doing the right thing for the wrong reasons still gets results in the end.

Not surprisingly, considering it's pretty simple, consumer action is a hugely popular form of activism. Boycotts not only put the economic pinch on companies until they take action, but they are also a great way to bring attention to a cause. In the UK, it's estimated that over a fifth of consumers have boycotted a brand over bad press. Non-activists are quick to get on board because while these campaigns illustrate how they might be inadvertently contributing to an issue (say, buying biscuits made with palm oil), they also offer a simple solution. Often, you're not asking anyone to do anything more complicated than switch brands.

Letter-writing campaigns

Typically, letter-writing campaigns are organised and coordinated efforts that ask a group of people to write a letter (ok, or an email) to a decision-maker. They're usually directed at politicians, government agencies or large organisations, like media companies or global brands. In a lot of ways, letter-writing campaigns are similar to street protests in that they're a physical show of support. Just like it's hard to ignore an issue if you can't move through a street blocked with protesters, you can't pretend it's business as usual if your desk is piled with envelopes from impassioned citizens.

While a protest (usually) lasts a day or two, and only involves activists who can physically get to a specific place, letter-writing campaigns can extend for years and involve people from all over the world. The flexibility of letter-writing actions means anyone can participate, making them one of the most accessible forms

 **EXPLAINER**

Amnesty International's Write for Rights

Write for Rights is a yearly project run by Amnesty International that asks people from all around the world to take part in letter-writing campaigns centred on human rights issues impacting communities at home and abroad. Each December the project puts two missions to participants: first it asks them to write letters to individuals whose lives and freedoms are threatened, to show that they're not alone and that people stand with them. Then it also encourages participants to contact authorities and demand they take action to confront a broad range of injustices.

Some people take part alone, while others organise mass events where participants can come together to write letters and emails, sign petitions and share the project on social media. To date, Write for Rights has involved people from over 170 countries, working across 6 million actions, making it one of the largest human rights events in the world. Its efforts have seen political prisoners released, death sentences lifted and governments forced to take action.

 # ACTION

Investigate the brands you love

It can be hard to constantly think about the ethical implications of what we buy, so put some time aside to do a one-time personal audit. Walk around your house and take note of the brands and products you use and purchase regularly. Once you have an idea of what you're spending your money on, research the companies' ethics, practices and history. If you don't like what you learn, think about how vital that product really is. Could you go without it? Or is there an alternative brand that aligns more closely with your values?

If you decide to make a switch, let the original brand know about it. Write them an email saying they've lost a customer. It's not only important to support responsible brands, but also to make sure that more problematic ones know their bad practices are losing them business.

Boycott v buycott

It's not uncommon to see activists advocating boycotting or buycotting particular brands, but what's the difference? A boycott is when you choose to not engage with a brand or service because you don't agree with their values or actions. A buycott is when you decide to take your business to a brand or service because you like what they stand for. Taking your money out of a bank that invests in fossil fuels is a boycott; moving it to a bank with an ethical investment policy is a buycott.

of activism. They're not limited by time, place or accessibility. If you have five minutes spare in your day, you can write a letter about a cause that matters to you. That simplicity is central to the power of these campaigns: they don't ask much of participants, so have the ability to draw huge numbers.

Because of that, a well-organised letter campaign can drive large-scale change. In the past letter-writing campaigns have been used to free political prisoners, help people access government and health support, protect ecosystems, block funding cuts, avoid business closures and generate massive amounts of press attention.

But beyond scale, letter writing is one of the most intimate advocacy methods because it involves real human interaction. Letters give everyone space to express how they feel and are impacted. That can be hard to get across in a tweet or shouting across a picket line.

That intimacy means letters can also serve as important support tools. Not all campaigns are about *changing* something. Sometimes they're about showing a member of the community who is facing injustice that they're not alone, and countless people they may never meet are willing to work to help them.

Art and activism

One of the most valuable and powerful things about art is how it invites us into other people's worlds. Experiences, fears and frustrations can be hard to express in words, but art often taps into something more emotional and subconscious. Many of the issues we talk about as activists are so huge that it can be hard for people to visualise and relate to them. But art breaks away from that by asking how you *feel*, rather than what you think. Activism can often mean spending a lot of time in your own head, so it's a relief to find more creative ways to share and consume ideas.

American artist Chris Jordan understands this connection, which is why he uses his art practice to help people engage with dry statistical information by expressing huge numbers visually. For example, one of his abstract images looks like a series of horizontal white lines. But the lines are in fact the rims of rows and rows of paper cups stacked on top of each other: all up representing the 410,000 disposable hot-beverage cups thrown away every 15 minutes in the US.

Art also brings us closer to issues that might feel far away. At the beginning of the 20th century, Jacob A. Riis's photographs of New York City's crowded and disease-racked slums brought the issue of safe housing to millions of people. Many viewers of the work would never have encountered the people living in these dangerous conditions. But the images were so shocking and heartbreaking they compelled people to act. Riis's work eventually inspired the city's residents, some of whom held social and political power, to demand large-scale social support and reform.

This century, the rise of the internet and social media has made the links between art and activism stronger than ever. Many artists use platforms like Instagram and Twitter to start new conversations with new people. Photographer Petra Collins has drawn an almost one-million-strong Instagram following for her dreamy photos inspired by teen nostalgia. But within her regrammable content an ongoing dissection of beauty ideals and gender roles is taking place, and she uses the platform to put out calls to get involved with other activist efforts she's passionate about. In this way, artists can turn initial aesthetic interest in their work into a chance to share about the issues that inspired it. It's a fresh point of connection that's not overwhelming.

They're not asking someone to read a pile of books or sit through a lecture to understand a point of view. Just to look at an object and examine how it makes them feel.

 # EXPLAINER

Guerrilla Girls are fighting sexism with art

The Guerrilla Girls are an anonymous collective of feminist artists who are committed to standing up to sexism and racism within the fine art world. They got their start in 1985, following the opening of *An International Survey of Recent Painting and Sculpture* at the Museum of Modern Art in New York. The exhibition was publicised as a representation of the international art world, but the Guerrilla Girls pointed out that of the 169 artists included, only 13 were women and none were people of colour – hardly a picture of the vibrant and diverse creative scene they existed within.

In response, the group created their now iconic street posters and stickers, which present statistics on representation in major galleries in bold and provocative style. To keep their identities secret, members wore masks and worked under the names of other female artists, such as Frida Kahlo and Käthe Kollwitz. The group's work now includes performance, books and billboards. Their focus has also expanded to include wealth disparity within the art world and the damaging presence of billionaire art collectors.

They now regularly show in many major galleries and festivals, including the Tate Modern and the Venice Biennale. Despite that success, the Guerrilla Girls are committed to remaining anonymous and not allowing themselves to be absorbed into the systems they oppose. Speaking to *The Guardian* in 2015, a member going by Zubeida Agha (named for the Pakistani artist) stressed: 'Galleries ask to represent us. But we're not interested in being part of the market and producing a precious commodity. You can buy our posters online for $20'.

 **EXPLAINER**

How the Nike boycott changed a whole industry

In the '90s, athletic apparel giant Nike faced a worldwide boycott that was so effective it transformed the company, the industry and how huge corporations thought about their global responsibility. The company came under fire for mistreatment of the factory workers making their products in China and Indonesia. As activists and journalists exposed the realities for these underpaid and overworked employees, the public responded by protesting and boycotting the brand. Faced with catastrophic economic and PR consequences, Nike was forced to respond and correct their labour practices.

In 1998 then-CEO Phil Knight infamously admitted: 'The Nike product has become synonymous with slave wages, forced overtime, and arbitrary abuse...I truly believe the American consumer doesn't want to buy products made under abusive conditions'. In the wake of his statement the company committed to raising their minimum wage, increasing factory monitoring and enforcing clean air standards. They also began performing audits of conditions and pay, and publicly publishing their findings to ensure added transparency and accountability.

The company's response was by no means perfect, and they still faced criticism over their commitment to transparency, but these actions were a huge improvement. The consumer outcry, and resulting financial impact, also brought attention to the practices of Nike's competitors. Ultimately, the boycott led to industry-wide calls to engage seriously with workers' rights and protections.

Never doubt that
a small group of
THOUGHTFUL,
COMMITTED
CITIZENS can change
the world. Indeed, it
is the **ONLY** thing
that ever has ✳

Margaret Mead

'Slacktivism'

We've already talked about how our online lives can enrich our activism. It's impossible to imagine 21st-century resistance without a smartphone in hand, and as digital campaigns and actions have grown, so has the backlash against online activism – sometimes disparagingly called slacktivism. Critics of digital activism often question how powerful Facebook updates, tweets and online petitions really are. They might be easy ways to engage with causes, but are they doing much good beyond making you feel involved?

As we have seen, successful movements use lots of different approaches, branching across physical and digital actions, to create lasting impacts. Disrupting normal routines through protests, strikes, pickets and sit-ins is a way to demand immediate action and grab people's attention. These projects are hard work, complicated and sometimes dangerous. The stakes are high when you put your body on the line. But that's also one of the reasons why physical actions work. Online campaigns are easier to start and engage in, but they're also easier to ignore. A bunch of mentions on Twitter isn't as motivating as having a crowd of people outside your workplace.

Sometimes, even well-intentioned digital efforts can go off course, especially when they become removed from the organisers' original intentions. That's what happened with the Black Square campaign during the 2020 Black Lives Matter protests. After days of organising following the killing of George Floyd by Minneapolis police officer Derek Chauvin, music-industry veterans Jamila Thomas and Brianna Agyemang put a call out to their professional community.

Posting on Instagram they wrote: 'We are tired and can't change things alone. This is a call to action for those of us who work in music/entertainment/show business to pause on Tuesday, June

 # EXPLAINER

How Milo Cress took down single-use plastics

Sometimes it's hard to see how actions in our own lives can make a real, large-scale difference. But Milo Cress from Vermont in the United States is an example of how a simple change can inspire countless others. When Milo was eight years old, he wondered how many plastic drinking straws were being used every day. He was shocked by what he found. While environmentalists have struggled to settle on an exact number, it's accepted that globally we're throwing away millions and millions of plastic straws a day – the vast majority of which end up as trash, polluting the planet and harming wildlife.

Milo decided to do something about it, so he founded the Be Straw Free project, which encouraged restaurants to give up plastic straws or provide reusable options. The call caught on, and what began as an observation eventually inspired countless people and organisations around the world to question their reliance on single-use plastics.

Almost a decade later it's impossible to estimate how many straws have been taken out of circulation. But the impact on consumer behaviour is clear, as individuals and businesses impose sweeping changes to shift to reusable and biodegradable packaging options. Speaking to influential US broadcaster NPR a few years after the launch of his project, Milo reflected: 'The reason that I focused on straws in particular is because for me, it was one step that I could take as a kid...I could encourage my friends...and when my friends started doing it, I think they felt really empowered not only to use fewer plastic straws, but to approach plastics throughout their lives with a different viewpoint'.

 **ACTION**

Start a letter-writing group

Being so accessible, letter-writing groups are an inclusive and welcoming way to engage with new and existing members of your activist community. Letters (or emails) are most effective when used as part of a well-planned, wider campaign strategy. They are a good representation of how many people feel strongly about an issue, and can put pressure on decision-makers.

All you need to organise a letter-writing day with your friends are paper, envelopes, pens, stamps – or just your laptops, phones or tablets. To make things easier, you can create a template or basic guide for people to follow. This can help them decide what they want to say in their own piece of writing. If you get stuck, talk to each other about your individual feelings and experiences with the issue you're campaigning over. Sharing like this often helps get pens moving.

Here are some questions to get you started:

* What are you trying to address?

* What solution do you want to see?

* If that solution is unlikely, or will take time, what are some smaller changes that you can put forward in the meantime?

* Who has the power to make this happen?

* Who else could you petition or put pressure on?

* What does success look like to you?

* How has this issue impacted you personally?

2nd because the show can't just go on as our people are being hunted and killed. Use this time on Tuesday to come together and figure out how we can hold our partners, colleagues and companies alike, accountable to come up with and execute a plan that actively supports and protects the VERY CULTURE that it profits from. #THESHOWMUSTBEPAUSED'.

That action quickly went viral, with members of the public posting black squares to their feed as a sign of solidarity and to symbolise taking a moment to reflect on their own role within racist systems. Unfortunately, many used the #BlackLivesMatter hashtag, which had become a vital source of news updates and protest information, ultimately turning that whole feed dark.

While the intentions behind the posts were good, many pointed out that not only did they drown out important information, but as journalist Madison Malone Kircher wrote for Vulture, 'A flood of black squares wastes useful digital space that could be devoted to the real cause'.

The drawback of physically disruptive actions is that they require a lot of buy-in and as a result it can be harder to motivate people to get involved with them. While online efforts don't always drive the same level of change, they do drive awareness. That shouldn't be underestimated. Awareness is a foundational step in becoming an activist. After all, you need to hear about an issue before you can care about it.

Tweets, memes, YouTube videos and status updates often fall under the category of 'soft activism'. That term doesn't only refer to the type of work that goes into them, but also how they're received. It's tough to get people to engage in the denser parts of activist discussions. But these bite-sized pieces of online content can distil complex information into easily understood (and shared) morsels that people can relate to their own lives.

Even ultra low-lift actions like changing your profile picture to support a cause are a way to show solidarity with marginalised groups. As countries around the world debate legalising same-sex marriage, countless Facebook users have updated their avatars with rainbow filters as an expression of support for the legislation. A small effort like that might not be enough to inspire politicians to immediately retool the law, but it's still a broad display of community support. For an individual impacted by the issue, scrolling through their feed feeling dejected, the effect of so many people publicly signalling that they stand with them shouldn't be dismissed.

Also, as mentioned, not all forms of activism are available to everyone. Individuals with restricted mobility, who live in isolated areas or under authoritarian governments don't always have the option to organise in person. 'Slacktivism' might suggest laziness, but in countries where expressing an opinion online, or even changing your Facebook picture, can get you thrown in jail, it's incredibly brave.

It should also be acknowledged that visibility equals accountability. Making public statements about your beliefs, actions and behaviours pushes you to carry through with them. If you retweet about the environmental damage caused by plastic shopping bags, and you know your friends and family saw it, you'll be less likely to pick one up next time you forget your reusable bag at the shops.

Ultimately, no action should be discredited. There are multiple parts to a successful movement. They all work together to build momentum and drive change. The ability to adapt approaches also becomes vital when our preferred protest methods aren't available, allowing us to respond to changing circumstances and maintain our effectiveness.

 **EXPLAINER**

Feroza Aziz showed that soft activism can work hard

Social media has lead to some really ingenious new ways of spreading a message. In 2019, US teenager Feroza Aziz wanted to use the video platform TikTok to speak out about the detention of Uyghur Muslims in China. But she understood that sharing this content on the Chinese-owned app could lead to her video being removed. To get this kind of political content onto the platform, she'd have to disguise it as something else – which is how she came to present her call to action in a makeup tutorial.

In the 40-second video, Feroza begins by announcing she's going to show viewers how to curl their eyelashes. To any passing observer swiping through, nothing would seem out of place. But if you stuck around, you'd witness her pivot from talking about her lashes to urging people to pick up their phones, look up the situation in China, share the content and become politically active around the issue. She goes on to detail the oppression of Uyghur individuals in detention camps, all while continuing to work on her makeup. Watching without sound, it wouldn't appear to be different from any other tutorial.

Her method worked: not only was the original post viewed over a million times, but it made international news. Ultimately Feroza highlighted not only the issues in China, but also how young people are coming up with genius methods of using social media to educate and manoeuvre around censorship.

*Inherently, having privilege isn't bad...but it's how you USE IT, and you have to use it in SERVICE of other people

Tarana Burke

 # ACTION

Review your reading list

Books can be a great way to engage with new ideas, voices and perspectives. But it's hard to do that if everyone you're reading thinks, looks and sounds just like you. Head over to your bookshelf and consider whether you've selected books from a broad range of authors. What kind of voices are missing? Are Indigenous, differently abled, non-English speaking or queer individuals represented? If not, spend some time finding new writers to check out.

When issues or causes go viral, it's not uncommon to see a handful of books jump to the top of the bestseller lists. More often than not, these are by major, established authors. While it's always great to see writers being recognised, be cognisant of other creatives you could also be supporting to ensure the wave of attention doesn't just lift a handful of voices.

Don't forget to pay attention to where you're buying your books too. Where possible, shop at local or independent bookstores. Ideally you want to make sure your cash is supporting your neighbourhood or community – not a mega corporation.

Chapter Six

ACTIVISM *Is* Adaptable

How COVID-19 changed activism

Before the COVID-19 pandemic impacted every area of our lives, we were living through a historic era of activism and protests. Every day new mass movements were emerging, as people all over the world stood up to fight for change in their communities. Many historians believed it was the largest surge of nonviolent actions since the Second World War – if not in world history.

Then the global health crisis hit, necessitating wide-scale social distancing and completely disrupting activist culture. But it didn't kill it. Despite the new physical and mental challenges COVID-19 presented, activists showed an incredible ability to adapt.

Rather than losing momentum or perspective, people found new ways to organise and utilise their time. With physical demonstrations such as protests, meetings and sit-ins no longer always being options, other forms of activism sprang up in their place. As researchers Erica Chenoweth, Austin Choi-Fitzpatrick, Jeremy Pressman, Felipe G. Santos and Jay Ulfelder reported in *The Guardian*: 'In just several weeks' time, we've identified nearly 100 distinct methods of non-violent action that include physical, virtual and hybrid actions – and we're still counting. Far from condemning social movements to obsolescence, the pandemic – and governments' responses to it – are spawning new tools, new strategies and new motivation to push for change'.

Digital campaigns, letter-writing efforts and boycotts all proved to be effective ways to continue agitating for change while in lockdown. And in the months after the pandemic was declared, several efforts grabbed international news attention.

The Sunrise Movement used the time at home to focus on political phonebanking ahead of the 2020 US election, while Fridays for Future members kept up their weekly strikes by posting images of themselves with their signs on social media. Hong Kong's pro-democracy organisers even figured out a way to use the popular video game Animal Crossing to gather virtually and spread their message.

Following the tragic death of George Floyd in police custody, people from all over the United States and the world stood in solidarity with the Black Lives Matter movement. While thousands chose to take to the streets, others utilised social media to share their grief, condolences, outrage and personal experiences with police violence. Alongside the physical demonstrations, these digital efforts ensured the incident broke through the blanket pandemic coverage to become global news.

Powerful new groups emerged during this time too. In Spain thousands of people boycotted landlords by refusing to pay rents during lockdown. In Poland women gathered in their cars or (socially distanced) on bikes to protest the government's tightening of anti-abortion laws.

Beware of disaster capitalism

Activism is about long-term change. A lot of the work activists do is about benefiting the world in the coming years and decades. This is easily disrupted by a crisis as all-encompassing as COVID-19. When you're so concerned about the immediate health and safety of your loved ones and community, it can be tough to maintain focus on the future.

The unfortunate reality is that there is a historical precedent for leaders taking advantage of the confusion caused by such events to grab power and implement controversial policies.

While we're distracted, they're often not held as accountable for these behaviours.

This phenomenon is often called 'disaster capitalism' or 'shock doctrine' (the latter phrase was coined by activist and journalist Naomi Klein in her 2007 book of the same name). Both terms refer to individuals and organisations finding ways to profit from disasters and the resulting public disorientation.

Recently it could be witnessed in the US government dismantling environmental protections under cover of the pandemic, or mining company Rio Tinto destroying a 46,000-year-old Australian Aboriginal site to expand iron ore mining.

A chance to reflect

Inversely, massive social and cultural upheaval can also be a time for positive changes. When everyone is forced to consider the way they live, work and interact with each other, when existing systems fail and are redesigned, it gives us an opportunity to consider what we value, what we want to save and what needs to be reconsidered.

One of the most famous examples of this is the New Deal in the United States: President Franklin D. Roosevelt's response to the Great Depression of the 1930s, when the world was plunged into an economic crisis and millions of people were in debt. FDR created large-scale government employment opportunities and direct relief systems that not only got individuals back to work, but also led to the creation of longstanding government programs such as social security, legislation that supported unions and workers rights, and the development of infrastructure and public spaces like parks and gardens.

 # ACTION

Go easy on yourself

During times of crisis, it's natural to feel a heightened sense of responsibility for people around you. But it's also important to look after yourself and remember that you're navigating a traumatic time. Don't try to hold yourself to standards set during less complicated times. If you find yourself unable to manage your usual level of work, that's understandable.

Also, while values in activism are vital, it's reasonable that you may find yourself having to temporarily re-evaluate them. Lauren Singer, the environmental activist, zero waste advocate and founder of Package Free Shop, experienced this when her need for personal protective equipment and food supplies during the COVID-19 pandemic brought her eight-year streak of living plastic-free to an end in March 2020.

Writing about her choice on Instagram and online she said that overall, 'My main value and goal in life is to create large-scale positive change.' But she also understood that for that period of time, by using single-use plastics, she could be helping contain disease spread in her community. She reflected, 'It is not for the planet alone that I am fighting, it is also for the people that inhabit it…in understanding this, I realized that I don't have to abide by just one main value system. I have many values and sometimes, as circumstances change, one of those values may take priority above another.'

* I don't believe in charity. I believe in SOLIDARITY. Charity is so vertical. It goes from the top to the bottom. Solidarity is horizontal. It RESPECTS the other person. I have a lot to learn from other people

Eduardo Galeano

How to be an activist in a crisis

During times of upheaval, it can be hard for anyone to find extra emotional energy to put into anything – let alone something as complex as protesting. Plus, when the news is stressful and consuming, as it was with COVID-19, it can feel a bit awkward to ask people to divert their attention to other causes.

But remember, activism is a team sport, and often the social connection and shared excitement it provides is what helps sustain us through the tough times. In the event of disruption due to outside events, local or global, do your best to stay connected to your activist values, work and friends. If you are in a routine of meeting with a group regularly, keep it up, if possible – or stay motivated by attending online talks and meetings, as well as picking up the phone and checking in one on one. Even if you're not in a position to plan and organise, take the time to share your experiences and anxieties.

And if you do find you need to shift your priorities to other spaces for a while, there is nothing wrong with that. As the world keeps changing and new opportunities present themselves, the important thing is to ensure we're in a mental and emotional state to take advantage of them (we'll talk more about this soon).

Innovative activism

Activism has always survived and thrived in periods of change. This is when it is most vital – and often when people find exciting and inventive ways to organise, demonstrate and stand up for what's right.

Every day during the COVID-19 pandemic the news was full of protesters organising car caravans, cacerolazos (the form of protest where people collectively bang pots and pans together at home to create public noise), virtual events, mask-sewing workshops and even simply posting signs in their windows.

One thing to be aware of is how privileged those of us who are able to use online resources and platforms to make our voices heard are. As more activist work takes place online, it's worth being mindful of the fact that not everyone has access to social media and freedom of expression online. In countries such as Bahrain, Syria, China and Russia, online activism isn't so easy, and when the ability to safely show up and demonstrate in person is lost, as it was during the 2020 lockdowns, there are real concerns that voices will be lost.

This knowledge makes intersectionality, diversity and allyship more vital than ever. It also shifts more responsibility onto activists working in countries with freely available online resources to prioritise and promote a range of voices, experiences and causes beyond their own.

*

WE are the ones we've been WAITING FOR

June Jordan

When we're tested
by crisis we either
regress and fall apart,
or we grow up, and find
reserves of STRENGTHS
and COMPASSION we
didn't know we were
capable of *

Naomi Klein

EXPLAINER

The rise of mutual aid

One of the most comforting developments to come out of the COVID-19 pandemic was the emergence of mutual aid groups around the world. Mutual aid is a broad term that refers to acts of kindness and community support at a local level. It's often witnessed during crises when neighbourhoods and informal social groups come together to look after each other – usually when government or other official bodies have fallen short.

Mutual aid is different to traditional charity efforts as it's purposely not about handing out resources from top to bottom, but rather calls on people to help each other out as friends and equals. This grassroots altruism can take many forms. During the 2020 lockdowns mutual aid efforts included collecting and distributing food and supplies, organising child care for essential workers, helping older and vulnerable people with errands, and even supporting local businesses over larger chains and online retailers.

Chapter Seven

INTERSECTIONALITY

Is Vital

Together we're stronger

On 25 May 2020 a 46-year-old black man called George Floyd was killed by a white Minneapolis police officer called Derek Chauvin. Footage of the event, in which Chauvin held the unarmed Floyd in a chokehold while he begged to be let go and repeatedly said he couldn't breathe, went viral around the world. Within days Black Lives Matter organisers had begun leading protests around the country calling for Chauvin's arrest, but also standing against police brutality and institutionalised racism within the United States.

By the following week countless individuals in cities across the globe had begun gathering in solidarity and support, and flooding their social media feeds with information about police violence. Quickly these exchanges came to include international interrogations of state-sanctioned violence, the disproportionate incarceration of people of colour, and the lasting trauma of historic racism and colonisation.

The US protests drove conversations about the impact of racism on a global, national and personal level. Everyone was able to locate themself within this issue, whether as the oppressed or the oppressor, and this intersectionality is what gave the movement its world-sweeping power.

As discussed already, when looking back through history, the most successful protest movements have been those that engage people from all causes and sections of society. No action exists in a vacuum; all stands against oppression, abuse of power or injustice are products of the same broken systems.

It's the ACTION,
not the fruit of the action,
that's important. You have to
do the right thing. It may not
be in your power, may not be in
your time, that there'll be any
fruit. But that doesn't mean
you stop doing the RIGHT
THING. You may never know
what results come from your
action. But if you do nothing,
there will be no result

Mahatma Gandhi

 # ACTION

Think before you post

When a protest or social issue goes viral, it can be tempting to retweet and share every piece of content that you agree with. While there is undoubtedly value in working to disseminate trusted, valuable information, it's important to also pause and consider what you're adding to the cause on a larger scale.

If you found a piece of content valuable, then absolutely let others know. But make sure you also ask yourself: Why am I posting this? What value does it hold? Could this content be distressing to people impacted by the issue? Is this about the cause, or is it about me looking engaged? Whose voice am I promoting? How will I practise this value offline?

If the content is graphic, really question the wisdom of posting it. Sometimes a violent video or photo can shock people into action. But resharing painful footage and images can often retraumatise people impacted by the events. If you do choose to post, do so in a way that allows people the choice to see it or not. For example, post it within an Instagram gallery with a warning slide before.

Stay engaged when the noise dies down

Commit to a reading list, set up regular direct debits to keep financially supporting causes, join community groups or volunteer your time. Find ways to make activism part of your life, not part of a weekend.

It's not all about us

When we talk about activism, we're usually focusing on what we can do right now. We're looking for ways to organise, attend, speak and share. But this assumes we're working in spaces built around us, our needs and beliefs. So it's important to take time to pause and remember that activism isn't about individuals or being the centre of attention. Yes, there is power in fighting for the things that directly impact us, but we also have a responsibility to care about and protect causes that we don't encounter during our day-to-day.

That doesn't mean that it's up to protest organisers or leaders to convince us to care or show how their cause affects us – it's up to us to interrogate and recognise the struggles of others, to see how they are connected to our own and how we can work together to bring about change.

If we're here to create a safer, kinder, stronger world, then we need to guarantee it's safer, kinder and stronger for everyone.

That's where the question of what it means to be a good ally comes in. Being an ally means you work for causes beyond your own. It also calls for a different approach, one that asks you to step back, listen and support. In this role it's vital you don't try to force your agenda or ideas onto someone else, but rather are happy to be a body in a crowd for them.

Sometimes, slowing down, listening and creating space can be challenging. Especially when you're passionate and want to jump in. So when supporting actions that aren't your own, or that impact communities that you don't belong to, be vigilant about your own behaviour to make sure your presence is welcome and valuable.

Check your privilege and perspective

It's easy to sit by and agree that this all sounds great. It feels good to tell ourselves that we are selflessly fighting for the good of society together. But to fully understand that someone is oppressed by a broken system, you may need to admit that you are in turn being supported by it. If you're not being pushed down by inequality, you could be being pulled up. Even if you don't feel you are practising prejudice yourself, benefiting from unfair constructs still means you are involved and hold some responsibility.

Most people would agree that we need to create more space for, and champion, the voices of people experiencing oppression and discrimination. But for that to happen, many of us need to be willing to decentre ourselves first.

How to be an ally

You only need to spend five minutes on social media to see people reposting and sharing content and commiserations around issues that don't directly impact them. But while sharing information and resources is a good way to engage with your own networks, it's not enough. Being an ally isn't about not causing harm: it's about working for others as hard as you do for yourself. Here are some ways to start doing that.

Put your money where your mouth is: If you are in a position to give money to organisations working within causes, this is often a great first step. It allows people who are directly engaged with these issues to decide where resources should be relegated. But there are other ways to contribute beyond cash. Volunteering your time or expertise and sharing professional contacts are also valuable and meaningful ways you can help other people's actions.

You can also help people monetise their work simply by consuming it. Watching YouTube content or listening to podcasts created by people you support may allow them to make money through advertising.

Call it out: As we've mentioned several times, it's vital to speak about the issues that matter to you with people outside of your immediate circle. People often disengage from an issue when viewed through the news, but hearing about it from friends and family can help them consider it more deeply.

Also think about what spaces you have access to that others might not. That could include work. Our employers are often the individuals we know who hold the most power. Consider how the values you champion could come into play. It could be as simple as introducing a recycling system, or as transformative as creating standards about the clients and companies your employer engages with. When Mark Zuckerberg refused to take responsibility for violent and inflammatory content President Trump posted on Facebook, the social media platform's employees (who were work remotely due to COVID-19) staged a virtual walkout.

Speaking up to people – whether it's your parents or your boss – can be uncomfortable. But remember, if the worst distress you feel over an issue is awkwardness, you're getting off pretty light.

Show up: Attend rallies, protests and demonstrations. Show solidarity, but don't make it about you. Allow people central to the cause to stand at the front, lead chants and speak to the press.

Make a habit of calling or writing to your political leaders, lodge official complaints against brands and services who are complicit in prejudice or abuse, and flood their comments sections.

Don't forget to also be a good friend and neighbour. If you have people in your community affected by particular issues make sure you're always supporting, listening, helping out and being there when there isn't an audience. Resist the urge to bombard people you haven't spoken to in months with messages asking if they're

*

EVERYBODY can
be great...because
ANYBODY can serve.
You don't have to have a
college degree to serve.
You don't have to make
your subject and verb agree
to serve. You only need a
HEART FULL OF GRACE

Martin Luther King Jr

ok during a crisis or when something is in the news – this could come across as performative and cause additional stress. Rather, be sensitive to the ways the people around you are impacted by these issues every day.

Learn: Take time to educate yourself. Consume art, read books, watch movies and documentaries made by people affected by these issues. Many of the causes we're standing for today have existed for centuries. There is no lack of resources.

Revisit what you know about history and view it from different perspectives. Consider how western, colonial, heterosexual and gendered ideals influence how the past is taught and discussed. Again, it's your responsibility to do this, not someone else's to teach you.

Keep it up: When an issue is in the news, it's on our minds, making it easier to hold ourselves accountable. But be conscious of how you can make these values and behaviours a part of your daily life. Beyond giving money to causes, work out ways to build an ongoing relationship with them.

Understand that during this process you will probably make mistakes or face criticism. Don't be tempted to give up. There can be real growth from understanding and facing our own complicity and learning from it.

Being an ally isn't a constant state, or a level you achieve and maintain. It's a way of being, thinking and behaving that needs to be cultivated day in and day out.

 **EXPLAINER**

How the Paris riots began with students and engaged a nation

In 1968, students in Paris began protesting the university system, and the country's fixation on consumption and profit in the face of rising fears about unemployment and globalisation. When the original protesters faced heavy police repression they were soon joined by workers, farmers, small business owners and citizens from all over the city. These additional protesters understood that not only did the students have a right to demonstrate, but also that their concerns affected all French nationals.

That united force proved to be incredibly powerful. Authorities became legitimately concerned the demonstrations could result in another full-blown revolution. Eventually the protests led to the resignation of President Charles de Gaulle, as well as wide-reaching changes in attitudes and policy around gender, marriage, traditional values, sexuality, religion and education.

 # Allies Do

Listen	Educate themselves
Make genuine friends within movements	Admit when they're wrong, and listen to feedback
Interrogate their own privilege and biases	Turn up to causes, actions, protests
Learn the history of causes	Know the work is never done
Abandon preconceived ideas	Understand that trust takes time to build

Allies Don't

Assume they understand the broader context, or try to relate the issue back to struggles they've personally experienced	Ask people to do unpaid work (this can include giving talks or being on panels)
Expect members of a community to explain everything to them	Try to make others fit into their understanding of an issue
Want to be at the front	Expect to be thanked
Rush or expect to be welcomed into a movement straight away	Get defensive, lash out or blame others when they're corrected
Think they're always right because they mean well	Dominate conversation or speak for people

Chapter Eight

FEEL-GOOD

Activism

Activism and mental health

It's not hard to see why activism is good for the community at large. But it's worth also pausing to look at how it can be good for us on a more personal level. Philosopher-physician Albert Schweitzer once said, 'The only ones among you who will be really happy are those who have sought and found how to serve'. Translation: helping others feels good. We're living through a period of history that can often feel erratic and overwhelming. In the middle of all that noise activism offers a sense of connection, power and control.

In 1986, the National Institute on Aging in the US undertook a long-term research project to look at this effect more closely. They began by dividing 3617 participants into two groups: those who did volunteer work and those who didn't. The researchers kept track of their subjects over several years, checking in with them in 1986, 1989, 1994 and 2006 to compare their levels of happiness, life satisfaction, self-esteem, sense of control, physical health and depression. They found a correlation between volunteering and experiencing better mental and physical health, and noted that the social integration that came from helping others appeared to counter negative moods.

Decades later, Dana R. Fisher observed a similar effect while studying the ongoing impact that taking part in the Women's March had on people's lives. She said: 'Protests in this period have been used as a way to give people a collective opportunity for group therapy if you will. Which then helps to channel what I call the outrage that we see in the streets into actual activism'.

 # ACTION

Appreciate the small things

Surround yourself with reminders of why you've committed yourself to this work, and take time to appreciate them. If you're passionate about the environment, put a beautiful plant by your desk. If you're fighting for women's rights, keep a book or piece of art by an inspiring female creator nearby.

Commit to a non-activist hobby

It's important to create spaces in your life where you can de-stress and take your mind off your work. If you don't have something that you already love doing, prioritise finding a new hobby. It's ok to step back from actions to do things like garden, make art, cook, play music or exercise.

Break up the bad news

Bad news sticks in our heads longer than good. So make a conscious effort to not allow yourself to become overwhelmed by distressing facts. When learning about an issue, balance each piece of bad news with three pieces of good. It might seem like you're sugar-coating things, but really you're just counteracting the natural tendency to give stressful information a disproportionate amount of mental energy.

When I despair,
I remember that all
through history THE WAY
OF TRUTH AND LOVE
HAVE ALWAYS WON. There
have been tyrants and
murderers, and for a time,
they can seem invincible,
but in the end, they always
fall. Think of it – ALWAYS

Mahatma Gandhi

Basically, by coming together to take a stand, people were able to transform their negative emotions into positive action.

That's not to suggest that activism isn't also hard and often stressful work – but rather that it's often a treatment for as well as a cause of stress. That's what Dr Patrick Kennedy-Williams, a clinical psychologist from the UK, discovered when treating climate scientists and researchers at Oxford University. His patients were understandably exhausted by their work, and suffering from what's often called 'climate anxiety' – chronic stress over the state of the planet. Speaking to *The Guardian* he mused: 'The positive thing from our perspective as psychologists is that we soon realised the cure to climate anxiety is the same as the cure for climate change – action. It is about getting out and doing something that helps'.

There is a very real physical explanation for all this. When we do good things or offer acts of kindness, our brains release dopamine, oxytocin and serotonin. These hormones and chemicals work together to regulate our mood, promote a sense of wellbeing and lower our blood pressure. The unique combination is sometimes referred to as a 'helper's high'.

Beware of burnout

Unfortunately, the relationship between activism and mental health isn't always so sunny. This kind of work is undoubtedly rewarding, but it's also very tough and can expose individuals to extreme stress and trauma. Both direct activism and online campaigns can lead to situations where people's personal safety and security are threatened. But even when they're not in the direct line of fire, activists are at risk of experiencing vicarious trauma, compassion fatigue and burnout.

Work of this type can feel endless. By its nature, activism is never done. There is always another cause that needs championing, and that can become overwhelming. Reflecting on the climate scientists and researchers he treated in Oxford, Dr Patrick Kennedy-Williams observed: 'These were people who were essentially facing a barrage of negative information and downward trends in their work...and the more they engaged with the issue, the more they realised what needed to be done – and the more they felt that was bigger than their capacity to enact meaningful change'.

It means a GREAT
DEAL to those who
are oppressed to
know that they are
not alone. NEVER
let anyone tell you
that what you are
doing is insignificant

Desmond Tutu

 # EXPLAINER

Elyse Fox is changing the conversation around social media and mental health

While social media is often criticised for its destructive effects on mental health, activist Elyse Fox proves it can also provide safe spaces for people to connect and talk freely about their feelings and struggles. Elyse founded Sad Girls Club, a project that describes its work as 'Creating community in the mental health world & igniting conversations with GenZ & millennials', on Instagram in 2017.
Sad Girls Club places particular focus on giving space to the experiences of women of colour, who are often left out of mainstream dialogues about mental health. The online community is not only a supportive environment, but also a way to combat stigma and create visibility. On the Sad Girls Club's Instagram feed Elyse shares positive messages and advice, spotlights members sharing their own experiences, and provides resources for ongoing support. Since its launch, Sad Girls Club has grown from an online platform to a real-life community with three central goals:

* Remove the negative stigma integrated in mental health conversations.

* Provide mental health services to girls who do not have access to therapy and treatment.

* Create safe spaces in real life that build a community for young women to know they are not alone.

How to look after yourself while looking after the world

Self-care is an ongoing process within activism, and it's important to create space within your work to breathe, reflect and occasionally step away. By looking after yourself, and sometimes shifting focus, you can ensure your long-term wellbeing and engagement. Pace yourself, connect with others and explore the parts of activist culture that you find most nourishing.

Slow down and shift your perspective: Activism isn't a sprint; it's a multi-generational relay. So don't expect things to happen fast or fall into the trap of feeling like everything is your responsibility. Some things may take decades to change, and that's ok. Also, be willing to accept that some actions might not play out exactly how you want them to. Actions don't need to be perfect to be impactful.

Focus on long-term goals as well as short-term victories, and allow yourself to celebrate your achievements.

Lean on others: As we've mentioned, community and networks are vital within activism. But never more so than when you're struggling. If you're feeling overwhelmed, reach out to the people around you and let them know. This isn't all on you, so don't carry the burden alone. Also, chances are others are going, or have been, through similar experiences. By talking about it you can help each other feel supported, and reinforce the belief that these feelings are normal and should be shared.

Unplug to recharge: Although it might seem counterintuitive, working constantly is the worst thing you can do for productivity. All it does is bring you to a breaking point where you feel too stressed out to actually get anything meaningful done.

There are several ways to manage and prevent burnout in the short and long term. Each day, take time to pause and appreciate what you have achieved, even if it's sending a few emails or organising a meeting. Don't fall into the trap of feeling like you should always be starting another task.

Allow yourself time to step out of the activism headspace. Make sure you have other hobbies and interests: exercise, go for walks, visit museums, read books, enjoy art, cook. You're doing this work to make the world a better place, but you still need to find time to enjoy it.

While that all sounds simple, it can be deceptively tough. Sometimes unplugging, turning off the news or allowing yourself to get caught up in less serious things can leave you feeling guilty. Know that these moments of respite are as vital as any direct action. They allow you to recharge so you can remain committed to your work.

Take time out if you need to: If you're feeling burnt out or exhausted, there are many ways to get back to your old self, and they'll differ from individual to individual. But one thing to watch out for and avoid is the sense that you just need to work harder and longer to eventually conquer your endless to-do list. That never works. The only way out of feeling trapped is to change directions: whether that means slowing down, finding a new way to engage with your cause or stopping altogether for a while.

Lifelong activists often talk about finding ways to adapt their involvement over the years. Many step in and out of traditional actions and discover alternative ways to support their community. Not everyone can be, or needs to be, on the front lines. Social change is a lot of work. It requires teachers, doctors, lawyers, academics, farmers, food providers, scientists, parents and countless others to help spread the message. If you find yourself gravitating towards a less direct role, it's not a failure. It's just a way to use your skills and experience in a different way.

Whichever road you take to recovery, it can sometimes feel like things will never go back to normal, but with a bit of rest and time away your body and mind will demonstrate a phenomenal ability to repair, revive and rekindle your passion for this work.

If you are NEUTRAL in situations of injustice, you have chosen the side of the OPPRESSOR *

Desmond Tutu

Learn from your discomfort: While it's vital that activists look after their own mental and physical health, it's important to acknowledge that this work should be uncomfortable at times. When we're fighting oppressive and destructive systems, we may be forced to examine our own roles within them. As we learn more, we will very likely begin to review past behaviours and realise we've made mistakes too. Remember: we can learn a lot from situations that make us uncomfortable.

Many activists talk about experiencing periods of extreme personal guilt and shame – especially early in their work when they're beginning to unpack their own behaviour and impact. This process is an opportunity for real growth – but you need to stick with it.

It's easy to fall into a spiral of shame, exhaustion, denial and avoidance that can eventually lead you out of activist spaces. But guilt doesn't equal action. While feeling bad is part of the process, it's not helping anyone who is directly affected by the issues you are engaging with. Face your discomfort, interrogate what it says about you and use it to find ways to improve. Allow it to make you more empathetic, and revisit the values you were encouraged to outline at the beginning of this book. Stay focused on them and the larger outcomes you're fighting for; understand that they're much bigger than your individual stress. Take time to rest and refocus, but lose sight of what you're here for.

 **EXPLAINER**

What is vicarious trauma?

You don't need to be directly involved in an event to be impacted by it. Trauma can be experienced second-hand – for example, when hearing about a situation or how it has impacted others. This is often called vicarious trauma, and it's a very real issue for activists working in frontline roles that require them to speak to and support individuals who have experienced extreme hardship.

What is compassion fatigue?

Even the most caring people in the world don't have endless resources of emotional energy. Over time, it's human to experience a reduced capacity to feel empathy for people you're working directly or indirectly with. Compassion fatigue can present as emotional apathy, or a lack of motivation to step in and help.

What is burnout?

Burnout usually refers to a deep emotional, physical and mental exhaustion that can lead to a reduced sense of personal connection to in work that once felt meaningful. It often occurs after a period of extreme stress or busyness. The American Institute of Stress explains that it can come about in four stages: enthusiasm, stagnation, frustration and apathy. Vicarious trauma, compassion fatigue and burnout often intersect and can exist together. For example, burnout may involve elements of vicarious trauma and compassion fatigue.

Conclusion

No text on activism can ever be exhaustive: we're constantly learning about the world around us and how our actions impact others. This book was written during one of the most volatile periods in modern history. Every day I found myself revising what I had previously written because breaking news had changed the context and reality of the work so far, teaching me something new or offering a different perspective.

By the time you're reading this, the world will be different again. Some of the examples and observations made here might feel like they're from a different time. Which is why I encourage you to use this book as a loose guide, but not a final map. The most important thing is that you stay committed to growing your understanding of issues. Listen carefully to the people around you when they speak about how causes and events impact them. Respect their feelings, know they're real and don't dismiss them if they're different to something you've read (even in this book), or they make you uncomfortable. Activism is always evolving; make sure you evolve with it.

Finally, this book was written on the lands of the Wurundjeri people. I want to acknowledge them as the custodians of the land and pay my respects to their Elders past and present, as well as recognising their continuing culture and the contribution they make to the city where I work and live.

More broadly, I want to draw attention to the work of Aboriginal and Torres Strait Islander activists, who I learnt a lot from while working on this book – especially Warriors of the Aboriginal Resistance, Seed and IndigenousX. If you are a non-Indigenous person reading this, I encourage you to consider how you can support the ongoing work of First Nations people and Pay the Rent in your own life.

Thank Yous

I didn't go into this book as an intensely experienced activist myself. Rather I chose to approach the project from the perspective of someone who is herself learning, evolving, and trying to challenge established ways of viewing the world.

Because of that, I leaned heavily on the perspectives of others. Across the research and writing process, many groups and individuals were incredibly generous with their time, ideas, and feedback. My own network of activist friends and mentors were invaluable when it came to discussing, debating, and inspiring the topics explored here.

In particular I would like to thank Briony Towers, Dana Fisher, Zeynep Tufekci, and Raven Cretney for taking the time to speak to me at the beginning of my research. Their perspectives helped my form the skeleton of what I wanted this book to be. Not only did their feedback and observations guide me where I needed to go, but their fair and constructive observations also helped me avoid missteps I no doubt would have taken alone.

Finally I'd like to thank my partner Ben and my family. Collectively they've created an environment when I not only always felt safe to speak up and out, but also showed me how powerful kindness can be when it comes to creating worlds and communities we're proud of.

Further Reading

As is probably clear from reading this, several organisations deeply informed the approaches suggested in this book. For anyone interested in learning more and becoming involved with groups creating change in local communities and around the world, I would wholeheartedly suggest you spend a bit of time on the following websites:

* seedmob.org.au
* facebook.com/WARcollective
* indigenousx.com.au
* sbs.com.au/nitv
* blacklivesmatter.com
* fridaysforfuture.org
* extinctionrebellion.uk
* sunrisemovement.org
* marchforourlives.com
* amnesty.org.au

Published in 2021 by Hardie Grant Books, an imprint of Hardie Grant Publishing

Hardie Grant Books (Melbourne)
Building 1, 658 Church Street
Richmond, Victoria 3121

Hardie Grant Books (London)
5th & 6th Floors
52–54 Southwark Street
London SE1 1UN

hardiegrantbooks.com

A catalogue record for this
book is available from the
NATIONAL
LIBRARY   National Library of Australia
OF AUSTRALIA

How to Think Like an Activist
ISBN 9781743796627

10 9 8 7 6 5 4 3 2 1

Commissioning Editor: Alice Hardie-Grant
Editor: Sonja Heijn
Design Manager: Mietta Yans
Designer: Ngaio Parr
Production Manager: Todd Rechner

Colour reproduction by Splitting Image Colour Studio
Printed in China by Leo Paper Products LTD.

The paper this book is printed on is from certified FSC®
certified forests and other sources. FSC® promotes
environmentally responsible, socially beneficial and
economically viable management of the world's forests.

Hardie Grant acknowledges the Traditional Owners of the country on which we work,
the Wurundjeri people of the Kulin nation and the Gadigal people of the Eora nation,
and recognises their continuing connection to the land, waters and culture.
We pay our respects to their Elders past, present and emerging.